THE ART
OF CONFIDENT
PUBLIC SPEAKING

Grant G. Gard

Prentice-Hall, Inc., Englewood Cliffs, N.J.

Prentice-Hall International (UK) Limited, *London*
Prentice-Hall of Australia, Pty. Ltd., *Sydney*
Prentice-Hall Canada, Inc., *Toronto*
Prentice-Hall Hispanoamericana, S.A., *Mexico*
Prentice-Hall of India Private Ltd., *New Delhi*
Prentice-Hall of Japan, Inc., *Tokyo*
Prentice-Hall of Southeast Asia Pte. Ltd., *Singapore*
Whitehall Books, Ltd., *Wellington, New Zealand*
Editora Prentice-Hall do Brasil Ltda., *Rio de Janeiro*

Library of Congress Cataloging-in-Publication Data

Gard, Grant G.
  The art of confident public speaking.

  Includes index.
  1. Public speaking.   2. Oratory.   I. Title.
PN4121.G26 1985   808.5′1   85-16980

ISBN 0-13-046897-5

Printed in the United States of America

CONTENTS

How This Book Can Help
You to Reap the Rewards of
Public Speaking

HAS THIS EVER HAPPENED TO YOU?

You Want Me to Give a Speech? No Way!

In September 1947, I enrolled at Kearney State College to continue my formal education. I'll never forget that day. My adviser had suggested that I take a class in English Literature, and so I registered for one. On my first day in that classroom, I received quite a shock. I was informed by the instructor that I was one of three students chosen to study a certain English writer's works and that I would be expected to give a ten-minute summary report to the class the following week. The instructor wanted *me* to give a speech? No way!

I immediately started to feel very, very uncomfortable. I began to have stage fright symptoms just thinking about giving that speech. My hands immediately started to perspire, I didn't hear another word spoken in that classroom that day, and I could feel my heart pounding. A feeling of emotional sickness began to creep in. All of my life, I had successfully avoided speaking in front of groups by making up excuses. Now, my inability to handle stage fright had caught up with me again. I couldn't escape from this talk . . . or could I?

After class was over, I immediately went to the registrar's office, cancelled my enrollment in the course, and registered for a class in which I was assured that I would not have to give a speech. *Fear had defeated me again.* Has an incident of this nature ever happened to you?

HOW TO END NEGATIVE BONDAGE

We Would Rather Believe Something Is Impossible Than Attempt to Do It

Five or six years later, after turning down many more opportunities to speak in public, I realized that if I ever was going to get any type of job promotion, if I ever was going to achieve my goals and ambitions, if I ever was going to have an inner peace of mind and happiness, if I ever was going to feel proud of myself, if I ever was going to be a success, I must immediately put an end to this fear that was defeating me. I must stop being negative and stop believing that public speaking was something I couldn't do.

Success Comes from Doing What You Have to Do, not from Doing What You Want or Like to Do

By this time, I was ready to admit to the world that I was plagued with stage fright, and I was ready to do something about my situation. As Jean Richter said, "Courage consists not in blindly overlooking danger, but in seeing it and conquering it." I clearly saw that fear was overpowering me, and now, at last, I was ready to conquer it.

One of the most difficult decisions I ever made was to enroll in a confidence-building public-speaking class. I didn't want to do it; I didn't like to do it; but I realized I had to do it.

OBSTACLES SHOULD CAUSE POSITIVE MOTIVATION

The Greater the Obstacle, the More Personal Glory in Overcoming It

Up to this point, I was a failure at public speaking, but as I look back, that was good. Why? Because it gave me an opportunity to turn defeats into personal victories. Due to those defeats, I developed an inspirational dissatisfaction within me, an inspirational dissatisfaction so strong that it caused an attitude change, a self-image change, a new meaning for the powerful words of *goal* and *self-motivation*. I became aware that obstacles and disadvantages can be turned into advantages and, when handled properly, can actually cause positive motivation. When I first started the public-speaking course, I was determined to be the most positive, the most committed, and the best speaker in the class. I was determined to *work hard* and *practice*. I told myself that nothing was going to stop me from turning "mental defeats" into "glorious personal victories."

Believe me, it was difficult to make those first few speeches. But the important thing was that I did it! And I kept doing it! Each time I gave a speech, it became a little easier, and each experience was a much-needed and welcome personal victory. I constantly kept my mind on my goal and I mentally saw myself positively succeeding. I prepared and practiced. Each time I prepared, practiced, and gave a talk, I would gain a little more self-confidence and enthusiasm. I never once thought about giving in to the obstacles.

HOW TO CONTROL AUDIENCE FEAR

Perseverance and Positive Action Make the Difference Between Failure and Success

My direct, positive action was making magical things happen. I was turning adversities into achievements and was now controlling fear instead of letting fear control me. I was proving the words of William Burnham when he said, "The most drastic and usually the most effective remedy for fear is direct action." I'm convinced that persistent, positive direct action is the *only* effective way to control fear and to turn adversities into achievements. No one can do it for you. I was thinking clearly on my two feet, saying to a group exactly what I wanted to say, and I was enjoying it. I had gotten rid of the *excessive audience fear* and had learned how to make the remaining fear work for me instead of against me.

HOW TO GAIN MORE SELF-CONFIDENCE AND DISTINCTION

Good Speech Habits Train Your Mind in Many Practical Ways

I never fully realized how many pluses could come from overcoming one minus until I tackled this problem. I found that all of the essential qualities that I used to become a confident and effective public speaker—the positive attitude, the good self-image, the goal setting, the self-discipline, the added self-confidence, the communicative skills, and the enthusiasm—are qualities to use in every phase of life. Public speaking is so much more than *just* public speaking.

I'm convinced that successful experience speaking to groups is the fastest and surest way there is to build additional self-confidence and that mastering public speaking is truly a genuine shortcut to distinction. I'm also convinced that good speaking habits train your mind for every phase of your personal and professional life.

I so enjoyed public speaking that I came to love the thing I used to dislike and I decided I wanted to make it my full-time profession. Consequently, for the last twenty-five years I have been working as a full-time national professional speaker and as a trainer in speaking, sales, and management. I have thoroughly enjoyed and loved every minute of my profession.

WHY MY PERSONAL EXAMPLE?

What to Expect from This Book

You are probably asking yourself, "Why did the author go into so much detail with his personal example in this introduction?" I did so for three very good reasons.

First, I wanted to give you, the reader, an insight into my experience to let you know that every technique, idea, or suggestion that I present to you is "experience talking." There is not one little bit of theory in this book. I feel as though I have made every mistake it is possible to make, and I want to save you the time and frustration of making these same mistakes. I want you to capitalize and prosper from my experiences.

Second, I honestly believe that every person who *wants* to become a confident and effective public speaker can. I have seen this accomplished by hundreds of men and women. Success or failure is solely dependent upon one's attitude.

Third, I want to share my inner excitement and enthusiasm about the many side benefits of confident and effective public speaking. Not only can you acquire the ability to speak in public, but that ability will give you a significant extra advantage in everything you do in your personal and professional life. That to me is truly exciting!

HOW TO MEET THE CHALLENGE TO GROW

You Must Work Toward Your Goal

Warning: There are no magic pills to take at bedtime that will give you "the extra advantage," the many rewards of public speaking, the next day. You cannot expect to read this book on Monday and become one of the nation's great orators by Tuesday. If you wanted to become a competent baseball player, tennis player, swimmer, or water skier, you wouldn't expect it to happen overnight. You have to work toward accomplishing your goal. You know your success depends on you. You have to steer your own course and do your own thinking, and planning. You have to put your own plans into action. Henry Ford said, "The great trouble today is that there are too many people looking for someone to do something for them." The secret of learning to speak well in public is dependent upon your self-discipline and putting into practice the simple rules and techniques that I have outlined in this book. With personal discipline, all things are possible—you can achieve a higher level of professionalism in your speech making and you'll successfully meet the challenge to grow.

Whether you are a man or woman in high school, college, or the business or professional world; a member of a community service or professional club or church; in politics, sales, management or agriculture; if you have a *strong desire* to meet the challenge to grow, to be a more *confident* and *effective speaker*, to reap the many rewards of the profession, and if you believe that obstacles should spur us on to greater accomplishments, go directly to Chapter 1. This book is for you.

1

CASH IN ON YOUR PRICELESS, HIDDEN ASSETS

*Obstacles are those frightful things
you see when you take your eyes
off your goal.*

HANNAH MORE

Dig the Well Before You Get Thirsty

HOW TO BE A TOP-QUALITY PERFORMER

What You Do When You Don't Have To Determines What You Will Be When You Can't Help It

Why should I become more skilled at expressing my ideas, thoughts, or concepts in a group meeting? You may be asking yourself that question now. You may very well be saying to yourself, "With all of this horrible, dreadful audience fear (stage fright) that I have, why should I go through all the torture of developing my skills and abilities to express myself effectively in front of groups?" Or you may be asking yourself, "Is public speaking really useful today?" Are you one of thousands of people who cite public speaking as their greatest fear? If you are thinking to yourself, "I hope the boss doesn't ask me to give a report at the next company meeting," read on.

Be Ready for Opportunity

As former Speaker of the House Samuel Rayburn said, "Readiness for opportunity makes for success. Opportunity often comes by accident; readiness never does." There is absolutely no doubt in my mind that what you do in way of preparation when you don't have to determines what you will become in the future when you can't help it. If you aren't prepared for opportunity, you'll never capitalize on it. In fact, unless you are prepared, you probably won't even recognize various opportunities as they are made available to you. What we see depends mainly upon what we are looking for. As we grow and become more valuable, we see and seek better and greater things. Luck occurs whenever opportunity meets preparation.

Quality, Not Quantity

Opportunity comes to those who are "quality performers" among many "quantity performers." Opportunity for distinction lies in doing ordinary things well. I know of no better way than public speaking to develop the necessary, ordinary, every-day things so that we can do them exceedingly well. I firmly believe what A. S. Weaver said: "A person cannot get out of life what he or she should unless he or she develops the ability to speak effectively in public." I have noticed, almost without exception, that the man or woman who speaks well is the person who is promoted to a more responsible position, who is happier and gets more out of life, who becomes an even more effective leader or salesperson. Repeating what I said earlier, *public speaking is so much more than just public speaking.* Good speech habits train your mind in many practical and useful ways that are extremely helpful to you in your personal and professional activities. The more you develop your great reservoirs of unused abilities and talents, the more valuable you make yourself, the higher up the ladder of success you will climb. The old saying is so true: "Water always, eventually, seeks its own level." To make of yourself less than you can be is a tragedy.

THE SIX DYNAMIC, POWERFUL BONUS BENEFITS OF PUBLIC SPEAKING

Definiteness of Purpose Is the Starting Point of All Achievement

On setting out to accomplish anything different and challenging, you must know exactly what will be your payoff—the benefits. It's only natural that you ask yourself, "What's in it for me?" To answer your question, I am going to list six dynamic, powerful benefits that have occurred in the lives of people who successfully learned to express themselves effectively in various types of group situations. Read them carefully so that you can develop your definite purposes, your goals, thus giving you the positive motivation to stick it out successfully while you are further developing your ability to be a more confident and influential speaker.

1. *Win important, favorable recognition.* History books are full of examples of people who were able to gain favorable recognition by effectively communicating their ideas in public. For ex-

ample: In 1863 at Gettysburg, two men addressed the audience. One was supposed to be this country's most famous and qualified orator, a great celebrity speaker who spoke for nearly two hours. He tried to prove his greatness by his lengthy speech. Even though practically every person has read about this man at some point in his or her life, it is doubtful if one person out of fifty thousand can recall his name—Senator Edward Everett.

The second speaker delivered a simple, dynamic speech that was about five minutes in length, but we all know his name and the name of his famous address—Abraham Lincoln and the powerful Gettysburg address. This example clearly illustrates the favorable recognition that can come from a simple, powerful, effective message. Abraham Lincoln knew the power of simplicity and of using well-chosen, one-syllable words. To gain favorable recognition from his listeners, all the fat had to be trimmed off. Seventy-two percent of that great address was made up of one-syllable words! Abraham Lincoln's recognition came from doing the simple things and using simple words, but doing so extremely well.

Adolph Hitler used speech to gain his recognition in building a strong following. He said, "I know that one is able to win people far more by the spoken word than by the written word and that every great movement on this globe owes its rise to the great speakers and not to the great writers."

One of our deepest cravings is to be important and to be favorably recognized. There are many opportunities for you to be an active contributor at various meetings, thus gaining yourself favorable recognition. To do this, you must immediately drop your membership in a club of which I used to be president and chairman of the board. It's called the "Silent Majority Club." This club consists of members who attend meetings and have all kinds of good ideas to offer, but who are afraid to stand on their feet and express their ideas to groups. They express their ideas to other club members over a cup of coffee on a one-to-one basis after the meeting is over and when it doesn't count. Then there are a few people who aren't necessarily afraid to speak up, but when they do everyone wishes they would sit down because they bore the group with their ineffective rambling on and on and saying nothing. Either way, these people have hurt their chances for winning favorable recognition. Chauncey M. Depew summed it up very well when he said, "There is no other accomplishment which any person can have which will so quickly make for him or her a career and secure recognition as the ability to speak acceptably."

2. *Become more influential, earn a promotion, better sell yourself and your ideas/products, and/or make more money.* Deep down inside, everyone wants to be influential and persuasive. We want to feel important and needed. Several times a day, regardless of our occupation or profession, we attempt to influence other people. Every person on the face of this earth is a salesperson regardless of his or her occupation. Parents must sell their ideas to children, to the Parent-Teacher's Association, and to the various important social, church, and community groups they belong to. Men and women are speaking up more and more about various civic and political issues. The doctor must sell his or her ideas to the patient, and the attorney must sell his or her ideas to the client. Business people must get their ideas across to the customer, farmers must sell their ideas to the public and to the various agricultural organizations they belong to, salespeople must sell their ideas and products to the prospects, ministers must get their ideas across to the congregation, managers and supervisors must sell their ideas effectively to get maximum production from their people, and politicians must sell their ideas successfully to get votes. I assure you that the person who *has something to say* and *knows how to say it* in an influential and persuasive way is the person who will make his or her personal and/or professional goals a reality.

Competition is keen for getting promotions, pay increases, and good jobs. The person who can express him- or herself effectively to one person or to groups and who can think on his or her feet almost always gets into a higher leadership or sales position, provided he or she is basically qualified with knowledge.

I am sure that you have been in a meeting at which a second-rate idea that was expressed very well completely defeated a first-rate idea that was expressed poorly. Even though the person with the first-rate idea meant well, the image created was less than first-rate. Such things are not forgotten by top management decision makers when it's time to consider people for higher positions. Bernard Baruch said, "The ability to express an idea is well nigh as important as the idea itself."

Let me ask you a question: What's the difference between a $75,000-a-year executive and a $15,000-a-year executive? Consider these key points when answering. To make this a fair comparison, let's say they both have the same degree of job knowledge and experience. First, the $75,000 executive is not five times as knowledgeable and smart as the executive earning $15,000 a year. Second, the $75,000 executive is not working five times as many hours as the $15,000-a-year executive. That would be impossible. From my observations, the big difference in the two executives boils down to their ability to communicate effectively with all kinds of people, either on a one-to-one basis or in a group situation. The better we become at expressing ourselves effectively in group situations, the better we communicate on a one-to-one basis. The $75,000-a-year executive is effective both ways: however, he or she places a great value on time. He or she knows that the more people that can be communicated with effectively at the same time, the better time is used. The $75,000-a-year executive knows that you can say exactly the same thing, in the same amount of time, to three hundred people as you can say to one person. The top executive places a high value on communication, and understands how select, well-chosen words will motivate groups (or individuals) to enable him or her to obtain desired results. This executive has learned to control audience fear and that it isn't any more difficult to speak effectively to a group than it is to one person. In fact, this individual likes to be speaking to groups because he or she has something extra working for him or her in a group situation—mass enthusiasm! Thus, in the same amount of time, the top executive has made him- or herself over three hundred times as effective!

For some reason, the lower paid executives think that talking to one or two people does not require special skill or particular preparation. This is not true. Many times I have heard the remark, "I can speak to one or two people, but I can't handle thirty people at once"; or "I can speak to three or four, but I find it hard to get across to forty." That kind of thinking is just an illusion. It's no more difficult to speak to forty than it is to one or two. If that person cannot communicate effectively to forty, no doubt he or she is not being as effective as he or she thinks with one or two. It's obvious that fear is not being controlled by adequate preparation. Effective communication is important in both situations. Without proper preparation to communicate effectively in both situations, the lower paid executive is going to remain exactly that. His or her problem is basically fear and lack of good communicative skills and it will remain a problem until steps are taken to correct the problem. Sooner or later, a person's shortcomings always catch up with him or her. In this example, it's the $60,000 difference.

The same thing is true of salespeople. As you become more effective in communicating with an audience, you become even more effective in selling your ideas and products on a one-to-one basis. Sales go up and commissions go up. Selling in group situations is challenging, but the more persuasive and influential you become, the more rewards you receive. It all boils down to this point: Those men and women who are confident and influential in dealing with people singly or in groups are the ones who are going to get to the top in any field of leadership or sales endeavor.

James Allen said, "You will become as small as your controlling desire; as great as your dominant aspiration." In training hundreds of men and women to become more influential, I have found that you must first influence yourself to do the things necessary to bring about your goal achievement. Then you will have earned the right to be even more influential with people. When you are consistently influential with people, you'll get a higher leadership position, earn a promotion, better sell yourself and your ideas/products, and get a better job and/or make more money.

3. *Build more personal pride and satisfaction.* There is a great amount of personal pride and satisfaction in sincerely getting involved in your company, community, service clubs, conferences, conventions, or church meeting activities. Personal pride comes from growing, from doing something we didn't really know we could do because of fear or an inferiority complex, or from doing something we have never tried to do. Satisfaction

comes from doing things that the majority of people will not do. Pride comes to people who do a good job of thinking on their feet because they stand out over the masses. I agree wholeheartedly with William Shenstone's comment concerning standing out and rising above your fellow workers, the group called "average." He said, "Men are sometimes accused of pride merely because their accusers would be proud themselves if they were in their places." After making a sincere, honest contribution, regardless of how large or small it may be, and getting genuinely involved, we enjoy a "real worth feeling" about ourselves because we have added to and have helped to make things happen rather than having sat back and watched things happen.

With personal pride, satisfaction, and involvement in job and personal activities comes the feeling of having the "right spirit." A man or woman of the right spirit is greatly interested and concerned for the good of the company, church, organization, and community to which he or she belongs. These outstanding qualities help men and women to springboard to higher leadership and sales positions.

I have travelled all over this country, worked with and observed people in many varied occupations but for honest, downright pride and inner satisfaction, I know of nothing that will compare to standing before a group of people and making those people *feel as you feel* and *think as you think*. It will give you a new sense of personal power and will make you proud of your personal accomplishment. You will be proud because you have done your absolute best. The person who has done less than that has done nothing.

4. *Gain additional self-confidence, develop a more positive attitude and a better self-image.* In order to be successful in expressing yourself in front of an audience, you must train yourself to be positive and to see yourself succeeding in every endeavor. You must not only be positive about yourself and hold a good self-image, but you must be positive about other people—the audience. That's why I feel as strongly as I do about developing your ability to speak in public. As you develop these inner qualities to handle speaking events successfully, you'll automatically start using these powerful qualities in

your everyday life and in your profession. I know of no faster or better way to gain additional confidence, develop a more positive attitude, and increase your image than by mastering the art of public speaking. Only those men and women who have the ambition and self-discipline to do simple things perfectly will ever acquire the skills to do difficult things easily.

Confidence breeds confidence. You can make your audience have confidence in you by acting and speaking confidently. The same technique applies to most situations in life. It is sad but true that many men and women of only mediocre or second-rate ability enjoy more success than others who have outstanding talents merely because they know how to act and talk confidently. No one wants to be around a wishy-washy speaker who acts and talks without confidence. That's why I recommend that speakers immediately train themselves to act and talk in a confident manner so that they win the confidence of the audience. If the speaker acts and talks as if he believes in himself, the listeners will certainly believe in the speaker. Acting as if it is impossible to fail is certainly a good habit to form and use in everyday living and working situations also. The more we act and talk like the successful speaker and person we want to be, the more positive attitude we have while speaking, working, and living, and the better self-image we have.

As a result of further developing these essential qualities, you'll find yourself meeting bigger daily problems and challenges head-on. Soon you'll be able to handle bigger decisions. You will seek out and accept more responsibility. You'll enlarge your horizons, aim higher, and have greater expectations out of life. With every speaking "personal victory" comes additional confidence.

All of this adds up to living a happier and more rewarding life because everything we do, or don't do, is governed by our self-confidence, our attitude, and our self-image.

5. *Become more enthusiastic.* Growing is exciting! You will become more enthusiastic about speaking, life, your job, and opportunities when you start to develop further your hidden abilities and once you have discovered more of your potential.

Conrad Hilton said, "Enthusiasm is a vital element toward the individual success of every man or woman." With each successful speaking event, you will step up the next rung of the ladder of success. The more successful speaking experiences you have, the more enthusiastic you become. Nothing can stop the man or woman who is filled with a genuine, enthusiastic spirit.

Professor William James of Harvard said, "Compared to what we ought to be, we are only half-awake. We are making use of only a small part of our physical and mental resources. Stating the thing broadly, the human individual thus lives far within his or her limits. He or she possesses powers of various sorts which he or she habitually fails to use." The more minuses (excessive fear-stage fright) we turn into pluses (confidence-success), the more disadvantages we turn into advantages, the more personal powers we habitually start to use in daily living, and thus the more enthusiastic we become. Franklin Field said, "Enthusiasm is self-confidence is action!"

6. *Prevent embarrassment.* There are two very embarrassing situations many men and women face. One is being asked to give a short talk, or report, or to express oneself at a group meeting and then, because of fear, making up an excuse that sounds good and turning down the invitation. The second situation is accepting the invitation and then not being able to come through effectively by having confident control of the situation. Either way, it's embarrassing and it's a situation that does not project a favorable and desirable image. Chances for personal recognition or a higher management, leadership, or sales position have been hurt because a bad impression is most difficult, if not impossible, to overcome. The way to prevent such embarrassment is to be prepared well in advance so that the situation never arises. *It pays to dig the well before you are thirsty.*

HOW TO SET WORTHY GOALS

Little Plans and Low Goal Setting

It's amazing how many benefits can be derived from doing just one thing and doing it well. Make a complete self-evaluation. Be honest. Look at yourself objectively. No more procrastinating. No more excuses. Figure out what your strong areas are. Figure out your weaknesses. Exactly where are you now? Exactly where do *want* to be?

I urge you to take out a pencil and paper right now and review this chapter on the six categories of bonus benefits. Sell yourself on their importance to you, how can you use them, where can you use them, when can you use them, what help would they be to you, and why they are important to you.

You may think of several more benefits. If you do, write down every one that would help you in your particular situation. This is why you should exert yourself to learn to speak well in public. Next, number your ideas in the order of their importance to you. Next, write down the exact date you will achieve your goals. Be specific as deadlines block out procrastination. Review your goals and make sure that they are worthy and realistic, something that will stir you into action. Little plans and low goal setting won't do that!

HOW TO ENSURE YOUR SUCCESS

No Rule for Success Will Work If You Won't

When you set goals, you are turning intentions into commitments, and commitments into involvements. Becoming skilled at effective public speaking is just like becoming a master of any other occupation or profession. You must be totally committed and involved or you will not succeed. No rule for success will work if you won't.

Practice and actual speaking make up the other essentials to complete your goal-setting process. (They are covered in detail in later chapters.) Right now, I want you to develop a complete list of benefits—things you really want, your goals—from confident and effective public speaking. Keep your mind on your goals at all times. Review them frequently. This gives you positive action and motivation. You must know exactly *what* you want, *when* you want it, and *why* you want it. When you know that and have a positive mental attitude, absolutely nothing can stop you from achieving your goals. You have ensured your success.

It It's Going to Be, It's Up to Me

In summary, you've got many priceless, hidden assets just lying dormant, waiting for you to cash in on them. No one can do it for you. I'll give you ideas and guidelines to follow to help you become a confident and effective public speaker, but you must get into positive action and do it for yourself. Devote earnest effort in setting your goals and sell yourself on the thing you aspire to accomplish. Make sure it is a worthy accomplishment for you. Throw your whole vitality into it. What's worth doing is worth doing well. To do anything well, you must use your head, your heart, and your enthusiasm. *Thought without action is as useless as action without thought.* Action is a must to make your goals a reality. Tryon Edwards said, "He or she that resolves upon any great and good end has, by that very resolution, scaled the chief barrier to it."

"GARDLINES"

1. What you do when you don't have to determines what you'll be when you can't help it.
2. If you aren't ready for opportunity, you'll never capitalize on it. It pays to dig the well before you are thirsty.
3. You've got many priceless, hidden assets just waiting for you to cash in on.
4. A person will not get out of life what he or she should unless he or she develops the ability to speak effectively in public.
5. Public speaking is so *much more* than just public speaking.
6. The six everyday practical *bonus* benefits of effective public speaking:
   a. Win important, favorable recognition.
   b. Become more influential, earn a promotion, better sell yourself and your ideas, and/or make more money.
   c. Build more personal pride and satisfaction.
   d. Gain additional self-confidence, develop a more positive attitude and a better self image.
   e. Become more enthusiastic.
   f. Prevent embarrassment.

7. Establish realistic, worthy goals with deadlines (little plans and low goal setting carry no magic).
8. No rule for success will work if you won't.
9. If it's going to be, it's up to me.
10. Thought without action is as useless as action without thought.

THOUGHT-PROVOKING QUOTES

A wise man will make more opportunity than he finds.
FRANCIS BACON

Small opportunities are often the beginning of great enterprises.
DEMOSTHENES

Great things are done when men and mountains meet.
WILLIAM BLAKE

Plant the seeds of expectation in your mind; cultivate thoughts that anticipate achievement. Believe in yourself as being capable of overcoming all obstacles and weaknesses.
NORMAN VINCENT PEALE

Wisdom is the power to put our time and our knowledge to the proper use.
THOMAS J. WATSON

Next in importance to having good aim is to recognize when to pull the trigger.
ELMER G. LETTERMAN

You come into the world with nothing, and the purpose of your life is to make something out of nothing.
H. L. MENCKEN

The great pleasure in life is doing what people say you cannot do.
WALTER BAGEHOT

The secret of success in life is for a man to be ready for his opportunity when it comes.
BENJAMIN DISRAELI

Cultivate all your faculties; you must either use them or lose them.
JOHN LUBBOCK

The man who grasps an opportunity as it is paraded before him, nine times out of ten makes a success, but the man who makes his own opportunities is, barring an accident, a sure-fire success.
DALE CARNEGIE

Whether we stumble or
whether we fall,
we must only think
of rising again and going
on in our course.
FRANÇOIS FÉNELON

Take the obvious, add a cupful
of brains, a generous pinch

of imagination, a bucketful
of courage and daring, stir
well and bring to a boil.
BERNARD BARUCH

A man is only as good as
the tool he uses.
GOETHE

2

FIFTEEN COMMON ERRORS TO AVOID

If a man has talent and cannot use it,
he has failed. If he has a talent
and uses only half of it, he has partly failed.
If he has a talent and learns somehow to use
the whole of it, he has gloriously succeeded and won
a satisfaction and a triumph few men and women ever know.

THOMAS WOLFE

Errors to Avoid

INSTANT HELP

When You're On, You're On!

Are you faced with the task of giving a talk, report, lecture, or seminar in the next few days? If so, time is short. Whether you are a beginner at speaking in public or are a more experienced speaker, you want some *instant ideas* to help you do your very best because you are fully aware that when you're on the program, you're on. You want ideas to help you avoid the pitfalls and costly mistakes so many speakers make. In short, you want the best, most condensed help I can give you in a single chapter to tide you over until you have time to read and study the contents of this book in depth. That's the purpose of this chapter. All subsequent chapters will provide you with everything you need to know to become a confident and effective public speaker.

ANYTHING THAT DOESN'T ATTRACT AN AUDIENCE TO YOU, DISTRACTS AN AUDIENCE FROM YOU

You've Always Got To Be Good from Start to Finish

You want positive feedback. You want the audience attracted to you. You want to create a first-rate image or you wouldn't be reading this book. I congratulate you on being a person who is genuinely concerned and who has the self-discipline to work and prepare so that you are good from beginning to end. *There's no second chance at a bad performance.* Yet, almost daily I hear speakers say and do things that distract the audience from them rather than attract an audience to them. These distractions cause the audience to form negative impressions of them as speakers.

HOW TO ELIMINATE NEGATIVE HABITS

Form Only Good Speaking Habits
and Immediately Eliminate the Negative Habits

Why, then, do men and women who have accepted the responsibility of giving a report, a short or long speech, or any type of address or lecture do and say things that distract and annoy an audience, or turn an audience off and waste the listeners' time? (If you have 100 people in your audience and you speak for fifteen minutes, you control 25 hours of people's time!) You have a tremendous responsibility as a speaker.

My work and observations indicate that there are several reasons why speakers do and say things that cast a sour note on their presentations. The following list is not in any kind of order.

1. Through *habit,* some speakers aren't aware of their annoying mannerisms.
2. Some speakers fail to analyze their performance correctly.
3. Many fail to read and study material on influential speaking.
4. Sometimes the speaker has a bad attitude about him- or herself, the subject, public speaking, and/or the audience.
5. Excessive nervousness or audience pressure grabs hold and thus makes the speaker say and do things he wouldn't normally say or do.
6. Some speakers actually seem to get their feeling of importance from doing or saying distracting and annoying things.
7. Sometimes a speaker's ego is so great that he couldn't consider that what he says or does is annoying, it's the listeners who are wrong.

For your success, it's vital to have an open mind and a good attitude toward self-improvement. That's the key to eliminating negative habits. Minds are like parachutes—they only function when they are open. Develop only good speaking habits and immediately eliminate any distracting or annoying habits.

HOW TO PROSPER FROM OTHERS' ERRORS

Experience Isn't Necessarily the Only Teacher

You've heard the old saying, "Experience is the best teacher." However, why go blindly before a group and make an error or errors just for the sake of experience when you don't have to? The answer: Prosper from others' mistakes. The nearest thing to a real experience of our own is to have another person's experiences brought before us.

One learns to speak by doing, but even though you think you know right from wrong, you have no certainty until you try it and then observe the listeners' reaction. When negative reaction is observed, it's too late to change that performance.

HOW TO BE YOUR OWN BEST EVALUATOR

The Audience Is the Judge, Jury, and Executioner

I want to save you from the frustration and sometimes painful experiences that come from facing an audience and learning by trial and error. I want to help you to develop a self-confident feeling as fast as I can. I want to show you how to become even more influential as rapidly as possible by teaching you to be your own best critic by taking advantage of my experiences and other people's experiences. *A person who isn't his or her own worst critic is his or her worst enemy.* These fifteen instant-help, instant quick-check points can help you to have instant success and to start analyzing every speaking experience. By studying these points, you will immediately start thinking about "What's right," "What's wrong," "What my strengths are," and "What my weaknesses are." It's only when you become your own best evaluator that you learn something from every experience, gain even more self-confidence, and become even more influential. You'll also start evaluating other speakers and you will profit from their "rights" and "wrongs." You'll gain a great amount of knowledge from even those who talk badly.

From watching audiences' reactions and listening to hundreds of listeners' feedback, I urge you *never* to be guilty of making any of the following fifteen common errors. Always keep in mind that the audience is the judge, jury, and executioner. Even though the audience wants the speaker to succeed, when the speaker is "guilty" of these errors, the punishment can be, and usually is, quite severe.

FIFTEEN ERRORS TO SHUN

No. 1. Start with an Alibi, Apology, or Excuse

Some common alibis, apologies, and excuses that are heard frequently are: "I didn't really have sufficient time to prepare this talk," "I really didn't know what a group of (X) would be interested in," "When (X) called me to speak on this subject, I wondered why in the world he or she asked me," "I didn't know I was supposed to talk on (X) until I got to the meeting tonight. I'll have you know that this came as a complete surprise to me. I'm sorry I'm not better prepared for you," and "For some reason, I'm not up to par today."

Alibis, apologies, and excuses are *negative*. That kind of mental garbage distracts instead of attracts. Such remarks turn an audience off and hurt your image far more than help it. Never start your talk on a negative note. This is true for even impromptu speaking. Webster defines *impromptu* as, "without preparation or advance thought; offhand." If you are in an audience and stand up to express yourself impromptu, offhand, or off-the-cuff, or if the meeting chairperson suddenly and without any advance warning asks you to rise or to come forward and express your views and opinions, the audience automatically knows that you are speaking impromptu. They witnessed the event. You certainly don't have to apologize and make up an alibi.

When the program chairperson calls you on extremely short notice and requests that you fill in for a speaker who for some reason couldn't fulfill his or her committment, the chairperson or the person introducing you should enlighten the audience that you are filling in on short notice. It's the chairperson's, or presenter's, responsibility to handle this smoothly and in such a way that he or she does not make you look like a second-rate or second-choice speaker.

You never know, however, what some introducer might say or what he or she might not say. You've got to be able to handle any situation that might arise on the spur of the moment. In the event that the introducer doesn't tell the audience the actual situation and makes you out to be "just another prepared speaker," you certainly are justified in informing the audience of the true circumstances. Be brief. "There's one thing our program chairperson overlooked telling you and I'm sure he wanted you to know. You can see by your program that I am not the scheduled speaker. Because of bad flying weather, our scheduled speaker's flight was cancelled. So about two hours ago I was asked to fill in." Move immediately into your speech. Don't add an apology such as, "So you can see I haven't had any preparation time and I don't really feel adequate, but I'll try." That apology doesn't add one positive thing; in fact, it belittles you. You are very knowledgeable and a respected person on the subject or you would never have been asked to fill in! A situation such as this comes up very, very infrequently, but it's best to know how to handle it in the event that it does. Again, the introducer should handle this properly and in a very positive way in your introduction.

I have found audiences to be extremely fair with speakers and to make an allowance, if necessary, for your short preparation time. I've even heard remarks such as this after the session: "Hey, Joe, wasn't that a great job Helen, our fill-in speaker, did on such short notice. She was better than some of our prepared speakers."

In summary, the audience is not interested in hearing your alibis, apologies, and excuses whether they are real or made up. If the speaker has to make alibis, apologies, and excuses for being there, he or she should do the audience a favor and stay home. However, it's interesting to observe how some speakers seem to get a feeling of importance by spouting out apologies. *Don't do it!*

No. 2. Be on an Ego Trip

James Thorpe stated it very well when he said, "Admiration for thy self is so consuming a passion that little may be left over for others." Letting the audience know that they are most certainly fortunate to have you as their speaker today is not an effective way of turning a group on. Some speakers have their human engineering rules backwards. Instead of facing up to the fact that the speaker has the responsibility of building up the audience and putting the audience on the pedestal, some speakers feel that they must build up themselves so that they are high on the pedestal looking down on and speaking down to their group.

Speakers have many ways of doing this. One way is through "name dropping" or "place dropping." For example, "I'm certainly happy to be here with you folks tonight as I work on a really tight, busy schedule. In fact, it was just yesterday that I was in conference at the White House discussing my views with the President," or "Last week I was on the platform with (X). I'm sure you've all heard of him or her. He's or she's the President and Chief Executive Officer of the XYZ International Corporation."

If these things are important and add to your bio credentials or pertain to the speech you are about to give, the program chairperson will be happy to include them in your speech of introduction, where they belong. Let someone else say those impressive things about you. It's far more effective than your "bragging on yourself."

Recently, I was a wrap-up speaker for the afternoon session for a convention in Wisconsin. The speaker who preceded me was a special assistant to the president of a new, fast-growing company. He told the audience in a most "holier than holy way" that his company was on a "fast-growth track." He was sure everyone in the audience had heard of his company's outstanding growth record and accomplishments because the company had "stepped on many toes" and would be "stepping on many more toes" of competitive companies to get where it wanted to go. Many of the "toes already stepped on or that would be stepped on" were companies represented in the audience. His entire twenty-minute talk was delivered in an arrogant, overbearing way. He was displaying great admiration for himself, showed little respect for his listeners, and talked down to the audience. The result? His image, and his company's image, sank to an all-time low. It's hard to imagine an executive giving a talk such as that with no diplomacy, tact, or good human engineering principles. The president of the trade association told me after the session was over, "(X) really killed the audience with his ego."

Never be on a self-satisfying ego trip in which you are over impressive. Your ego, actions, and words will kill the audience. Benjamin Lichtenberg said, "Stature comes not with height but with depth."

No. 3. Speak Too Softly and Too Far Away from the Microphone

There is no better way to aggravate, bore and annoy the audience completely than to speak in such a soft tone or too far away from the microphone so that you cannot be heard clearly. It doesn't take long for the group to yell, "Louder! Louder! We can't hear you." Where this has happened, I've seen members of the audience get up and leave unless the condition is corrected at once. I once heard a gentleman give the invocation preceding a banquet meal in such a soft manner that it was most difficult for those seated at the head table, where he was standing at the microphone, to even hear what he said. When he sat down, someone from the audience yelled out, "Have Jim do it again. This time so we can hear him." Practice will cure this problem.

No. 4. Come to the Meeting Ill-Prepared for the Specific Group

You certainly don't have to be a full-time professional speaker to make an effective talk, but you sure do have to prepare. It is rude and ill-mannered to come to a meeting knowing that you are a speaker and that you are not well prepared.

Frankly, it shows a lack of genuine interest in the audience. It shows that you do not respect the listeners. How can you expect the audience to be interested in you if you as the speaker aren't interested in them?

If you are not prepared, it will show on you personally by the way you look as well as what you say and how you say it. When you hear the applause at the end, it won't be appreciation for a job well done. It will be applause for stopping and drawing the experience to a close.

No. 5. Mispronounce the Name of the Group or Any Individual

To mispronounce the name of any individual, group, or company that you are addressing is nothing short of instant death. To do this is most embarrassing regardless of how good a recovery you make. To win over an audience you must be a practitioner of the best human engineering principles. Standing before an audience is no place to be testing your ability to pronounce the names of people and things correctly. That should be done before you start speaking.

No. 6. Make a Fuss about the Time or Your Watch/Clock

Some speakers go through a regular ritual or quite a colorful ceremony as part of their opener or sometimes they will hold off until right about the middle of their speech: "Now, Mr. Program Chairman, I understand you wanted me to speak for about thirty minutes. Are we still on that schedule? Just checking. By the way, what time do you have? I'll set my watch, because the last thing I want to do is to keep this group overtime."

Then the speaker picks up the watch or clock, winds it if it's the old fashioned watch or stop watch, looks carefully at it, and maybe even holds it up to his ear to make certain that it is running OK. Then, with showmanship, he places it back down on the lectern so he can see it clearly and continues with his speech.

What did that add to his or her talk? Nothing. What a waste of time and effort. All those details should have been taken care of before the speaker ever started.

This type of speaker will probably run overtime and then apologize for five minutes at the close of the talk for running over.

No. 7. Have a Sober, Deadpan Expression on Your Face

"Like begets like," said Professor Overstreet. If your speech is going to be a painful experience for you, it's going to be a painful experience for everyone in the audience. No one can build favorable audience reception while looking as if he or she has been weaned on a dill pickle. You, the speaker, set the pace for everyone in the room. If you don't act and talk as if you enjoy addressing the group, the audience won't enjoy you.

No. 8. Tell an Off-Color, X-Rated, Racial, or Ethnic Joke

Being a speaker does not give a person a license to tell off-colored, X-rated stories or racial and ethnic jokes of his or her choice. Don't fall into that trap. My cardinal rule is, *If in doubt, don't tell it.* If a story or joke doesn't add favorably to your performance, leave it out. You never know who's in the audience that could be offended.

I believe in lots of good, clean humor as one of the effective methods to open a talk and to keep the audience relaxed and enjoying the talk all the way through, but the dirty, X-rated stuff, or racial and ethnic jokes, are out as far as I am concerned. The guidelines for using good humor are covered in a later chapter. Read and study this material before you attempt to use any humor. What is hilarious from one person's mouth may not as much as get even one forced smile from another's. You must have the ability to use humor successfully or you will fail miserably. I've heard some speakers who didn't use a wise choice of jokes and stories embarrass the audience. It might be tempting to do it to get a laugh, but never be guilty of doing it.

No. 9. Be a Time Waster, a Rambler, or Stretch Out Material

Audiences can tell immediately whether or not you have a compact, worthwhile message to get across. The group will sense if you are sincere and mean business. If you waste time trying to get started into your talk, or if you are a rambler, and/or if you are trying to stretch out your thin material, the audience probably will tune you out and quite possibly you'll never reach the group even though you may have an important message somewhere later in your talk.

Never overlook this very important fact: *The shorter and more compact your speech, the better your chances for effectiveness and complete success.* The speaker who is a time waster, a rambler, or one who tends to stretch out his or her sketchy material is one of the worst kinds of speakers. It's amazing how many speakers feel that lengthening a talk guarantees it to be better. That is true only when relative, important substance has been included, and even then it should be kept as brief and as compact as possible. In the fourth century Saint Ambrose, the Bishop of Milan, wrote, "Let us have a reason for beginning and let our end be within due limits. A speech that is wearisome only stirs up anger." Once you've stirred up an audience with anger, they are difficult to win back.

Today, people are bombarded constantly with effective commercials on radio and TV that carry an impact in fifteen, thirty, and/or sixty seconds. They are used to being captured immediately with short commercials and to getting hooked and involved immediately in complete twenty- to thirty-minute programs. Radio and TV people know that unless they immediately capture the attention of the listeners, they either will tune to a different station or turn off their sets. Audiences will not put up with a speaker who wastes time. While they can't turn to a different station, they'll grow resentful and tune out the speaker. Always keep in mind that with proper preparation it is very difficult to make a bad speech out of a short speech.

No. 10. Have a Stinkin' Thinkin' Attitude

Some speakers think that they can play games with an audience and that they can hide their attitude. Wrong! No way! A speaker might fool some of the listeners part of the time, but he or she can't fool all of the listeners all of the time. Emerson said about speaking to an audience: "Use what language you will, you can never say anything but what you are."

The following story illustrates how attitude and inner feelings pass from person to person. Little Jimmy came home from school and Jimmy's mother said, "Son, sit down and tell me all about school today." The little guy sat down, and for about twenty minutes he told his mother all the details about school that day. One day the next week when Jimmy came home from school, Jimmy's mother was busy ironing and she said, "Son, sit down and tell me all about school today." Jimmy sat down and only talked about school for about a minute or so and started to go outside to play. Jimmy's mother said, "Son, what's up? Why did I get the short response from you tonight? Last week you spent twenty minutes telling me all about school and tonight you just barely talked for a minute. What's wrong? Why did I get that short response tonight?" Little Jimmy looked up and said, "Mommy, last week you really wanted to know all about school. Tonight it really didn't make any difference to you."

As the attitude and inner feelings of Jimmy's mother were transferred to Jimmy, the speaker's attitude and inner feelings are transferred to the audience.

While good word choice is important, the greatest thing in a speech is not just the wording. To make a favorable, dynamic impact on the audience, the speaker's attitude, spirit, and convictions play a most important part. Just as sales are contingent upon the attitude, spirit, and convictions of the salesperson— not the prospect—the audience's reaction to a speaker is contingent upon the attitude, spirit, and convictions of the speaker— not the listeners.

If you have stinkin' thinkin', the audience will too, because

they will reflect back to you exactly what you are sending out
... the audience is but a looking glass.

James Allen wrote:

> Mind is the master power that moulds and makes,
> and the man is mind, and evermore he takes
> the tool of thought, and shaping what he wills,
> brings forth a thousand joys, a thousand ills;
> He thinks in secret and it comes to pass
> environment is but his looking-glass.

Your attitude, spirit, and convictions automatically tell the
audience the way you feel about your subject and toward your
listeners. You'll get back from your audience exactly what you
have sent out—no more or no less.

No. 11. Emphasize Your Unfounded Claims and Opinions Instead of Facts

William J. Reilly said, "Straight thinking starts with facts.
Careless thinking starts with opinions." We all have heard the
speaker who lost his or her effectiveness because he or she tried
to ram unfounded opinions and claims down the throat of the
audience. A speaker loses the audience the instant he or she
ceases to be believable.

Webster defines *opinion* as "a belief not based on absolute
certainty or positive knowledge but on what seems true, valid,
or probable to one's own mind." Webster defines *claim* as "a
statement of something that may be called into question."
Claims and opinions are turned into facts only when they have
been proven and are accepted in the listener's mind without
any mental reservations.

Webster defines *fact* as "a thing that has actually happened
or that is really true; the state of things as they are; reality; actuality; truth."

Unfounded claims and opinions turn off an audience.
Make sure that you are in a position to prove any claim or opinion and turn each into an acceptable fact by offering the audi-

ence some type of evidence to remove all doubt as to whether a thing is true. Never state unfounded claims and opinions. They annoy an audience.

No. 12. Keep Talking After Your Scheduled Quitting Time

Ignoring the clock can easily reverse the audience's opinion of you, and rightly so. What right does a speaker have to completely upset a meeting planner's schedule? It is rude and inconsiderate. It not only upsets the meeting planner's schedule, but it can affect the hotel/motel's meal, coffee break and room cleanup schedules, the convention attendees' and spouses' schedules, employees' and managers' schedules, as well as other speakers' schedules. Just because you have been asked to speak for, say, ten minutes, doesn't give you the right to ignore the clock and speak for a longer period of time.

For example, I was to give a keynote luncheon speech in Biloxi, Mississippi, for a convention of about 150 members and their spouses. The hotel was scheduled to start serving 300 people at 11:45 A.M., and I was scheduled to speak from 12:30 P.M. until 1:15 P.M., with my flight departure time at 2:30 P.M. The last speaker of the morning was scheduled to quit at 11:30 A.M., giving the attendees fifteen minutes to meet their spouses in the lobby and to go to the luncheon room. The afternoon convention session was scheduled to start at 1:30 P.M.

It didn't work that way at all, thanks to a thoughtless, inconsiderate morning closing speaker. He started his speech on time, but talked an inexcusable thirty minutes overtime. The attendees in the session were upset, the spouses waiting for the attendees were growing more upset by the minute, and the hotel employees were furious because the food was prepared for serving at 11:45 A.M.

Since I was the keynote speaker, the convention planner requested that I not cut my talk short to make up time. I started speaking at 1:05 P.M. and finished at 1:50 P.M., getting to the airport five minutes before my flight departed. I heard the meeting planner ask the two afternoon speakers to cut down their talks in order to have the general session conclude on time. All of those delays and rescheduling were caused by one thoughtless speaker.

Even though he gave a good talk and had the audience with him up until his scheduled quitting time, he lost the audience during the last thirty minutes and the attendees had a very negative opinion of him. It's too bad that all of the negative comments couldn't have been recorded and sent to him.

If you don't stop when your scheduled quitting time is up, the only thing the audience probably will remember is that you are one of those speakers who doesn't know when to quit. Some good advice that applies to speaking or to any phase of life is, "Always leave at the height of the party." And always leave an audience when they still want more.

No. 13. Equipment Not Functioning Properly

The silence that comes from a microphone or any type of audiovisual equipment that has stopped working is nothing short of disastrous. A howl or squeal in the sound system is annoying and distracting. Usually this happens right at the opening of a session or at the start of an event within a session. In most cases, the problem could have been prevented by a proper checkout of procedures. Or, to hold the delay to a minimum, standby equipment or parts should have been on hand. We've all heard of the pause that refreshes. This pause, I assure you, is the pause that kills the speaker's effectiveness and the audience.

No. 14. Do Not Wear Proper Attire

Your appearance either attracts the audience to you or distracts the audience from you. Good personal appearance helps the speaker to be confident, influential, and successful. An audience assumes that a speaker who is neat and properly dressed has a neat, organized mind and thus a neat, well-organized speech. An unkempt appearance radiates a sloppy mind and sloppy speech! Never overlook the fact that the listeners judge the speaker's status, character, and abilities by his or her appearance. Never create a sloppy image.

No. 15. Close Your Talk Inconclusively

The speaker who uses closes such as the following is really finished in more ways than one:

"Well, folks, that's about all I have to say"

"I guess I better stop as I think I covered most of the matter"

"Next time, I think I'll be better prepared as I'll have more time to find out more facts"

"I guess I'm finished . . . (short pause) . . . oh yes, one thing more I forgot to bring in and I wanted to include is . . ."

You *guess*, or you *think*, you are finished? If you have to guess, or think you're finished, and positively don't know you are finished, *you're absolutely, positively finished!*

By saying "I see by the clock that I have to stop," or "They are signaling me that my time is up. Sorry I didn't have time to bring more information to you," you are implying that you are quitting before your speech is completed. Those remarks sound as if you only gave part of your speech and they leave the audience dangling, up in the air. If you are not finished when you see by the clock that you should be, or if you are not finished and they are signalling to you to stop because your time is up, blame the right person for your predicament . . . yourself! You have not adequately prepared your speech.

All of the above examples are inconclusive, inexcusable, weak statements. Closes like that will never win favorable recognition from the audience.

GIFTED SPEAKERS ARE MADE . . . NOT BORN

Your Potential as a Speaker Is Unlimited

Your progress and the potential that you develop depend on you and your attitude and how much you study, work, practice, and put ideas and suggestions into action without procrastination. By eliminating these fifteen common errors and pit-falls from your speaking experiences, you will develop your potential as a confident effective public speaker as quickly as possible.

These fifteen "instant help" ideas are for you and your use regardless of where you may be speaking. Use them in your church, college, civic or service club, professional group, company meeting, community affairs, conference, or convention, so that when you stand up to speak, your audience will listen. That's the goal of every speaker. Always. remember, gifted speakers are made, not born.

"GARDLINES"

1. When you're on, you're on.
2. Anything that doesn't attract an audience to you distracts an audience from you.
3. There's no second chance at a bad performance.
4. Develop only good speaking habits and immediately eliminate any distracting or annoying habits.
5. Learn from other people's experiences.
6. A person who isn't his or her own worst critic is his or her worst enemy.
7. The audience is the judge, jury, and executioner.
8. Never be guilty of making any of these common, distracting, and annoying errors:
   a. Start with an alibi, apology, or excuse.
   b. Be on an ego trip.
   c. Speak too softly and too far away from the microphone.
   d. Come to the meeting ill-prepared for the specific group.
   e. Mispronounce the name of the group or any individual.
   f. Make a fuss about the time or your watch/clock.
   g. Have a sober, deadpan expression on your face.
   h. Tell an off-color, X-rated, racial, or ethnic joke.
   i. Be a time waster, a rambler, or stretch out material.
   j. Have a stinkin' thinkin' attitude.
   k. Emphasize your unfounded claims and opinions instead of facts.

    l. Keep talking after your scheduled time.

    m. Equipment not functioning properly.

    n. Do not wear proper attire.

    o. Close your talk inconclusively.

9. What is hilarious when told by one person may not even get a forced smile from another.

10. The shorter and more compact your speech, the better your chances are for effectiveness and complete success.

11. With proper preparation, it is difficult to make a bad speech out of a short speech.

12. What's around you is you.

13. Always leave at the height of a party. Leave your audience while they still want more.

14. Gifted speakers are made . . . not born.

15. Your progress and potential depend on you and your attitude.

THOUGHT-PROVOKING QUOTES

It is a true miracle when a man finally sees himself as his only opposition.
VERNON HOWARD

Adversity causes some men to break, others to break records.
WILLIAM A. WARD

The pessimist's fault is that he is not gay enough himself to realize that the only lasting fun in life comes from what we may contribute to it.
WILFRED T. GRENFELL

Man's last freedom is his freedom to choose how he will react in any given situation.
VICTOR FRANKEL

Worry compounds the futility of being trapped on a dead-end street. Thinking opens new avenues.
CULLEN HIGHTOWER

To try is not good enough, you must succeed in this worldly contest.
WILLIAM FEATHER

The spirit that does not soar is destined to grovel.
BENJAMIN DISRAELI

Never promise more than you can perform.
PUBLILIUS SYRUS

Nothing is so fatiguing as the eternal hanging on of an uncompleted task.
WILLIAM JAMES

What makes for greatness
is starting something
that lives after you.
RALPH W. SOCKMAN

A man should never be
ashamed to own he has been
in the wrong, which is but
saying in other words,
that he is wiser today
than he was yesterday.
ALEXANDER POPE

Let him who wants to move
and convince others be first
moved and convinced himself.
THOMAS CARLYLE

In great attempts it is
glorious even to fail.
LONGINUS

Hustle is not work
but the enemy of work.
ARNOLD BENNETT

3

KNOW YOURSELF

Man often becomes what he believes himself to be. If I keep on saying to myself that I cannot do a certain thing, it is possible that I may end by really becoming incapable of doing it. On the contrary, if I have the belief that I can do it, I shall surely acquire the capacity to do it even if I may not have it at the beginning.

Mohandas Karamchand Gandhi

Know Yourself

THE TRIANGLE OF SUCCESSFUL SPEAKING

Three Key Requirements to Becoming a Confident and Effective Public Speaker

The three "musts" are:

1. Know Yourself
2. Know Your Speech
3. Know Your Audience.

This chapter will cover the first leg of the triangle, *Know Yourself*. The other two legs of the triangle will be covered in following chapters.

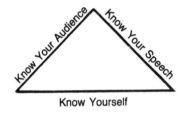

Know Yourself

HOW TO DEVELOP YOUR NATURAL STYLE

Don't Try to Imitate Others

You must be you. After observing speakers for over twenty-five years, I have concluded that not a single person who ever became a successful speaker was trying to imitate someone else. Each successful speaker found him- or herself and developed his or her natural potential to the fullest. It's important that you be yourself and that you never try to imitate others or be something that you are not. Denis Diderot said, "It is the man or woman who is cool and collected, who is master of his or her countenance, his or her voice, his or her actions, his or her gestures, of every part, who can work upon others at his or her pleasure." Yet I have found that one of the reasons why so many people dislike and fail at speaking to groups is simply that they refuse to be themselves. They refuse to look at themselves and their potential objectively. They hear four or five speakers and then try to imitate them. That's suicide! No man or woman can do difficult or great things who is not thoroughly sincere in dealing with him- or herself.

There is no one best way for me to teach you how to speak in public, but there is a one best way for you to speak in public. Yet the average person lives and dies and never finds it. He or she has been too busy trying to be something that he or she is really not. Sydney Smith said, "Whatever you are by nature, keep to it; never desert your line of talent. Be what nature intended you for and you will succeed."

I will share with you the basic ideas and techniques to use to help you to become a confident and effective public speaker. *You must use these ideas and techniques in your own individual way according to your own personality.* You are something unique, new, different, and special to the world. Be glad you have personal characteristics that no one else has. Develop and use them to the fullest. One who knows others is said to be smart and clever, but one who knows him- or herself is said to be fully enlightened!

Although Emerson wrote the essay *Self-Reliance* for the needs and problems of the people of his own generation, he gives stirring, worthy, and exciting advice to us in our present time. He wrote:

> There is a time in every man's education when he arrives at the conviction that envy is ignorance; that imitation is suicide; that he must take himself for better, for worse, as his portion; that though the wide universe is full of good, no kernel of nourishing corn can come to him but through his toil bestowed on that plot of ground which is given him to till. The power which resides in him is new in nature, and none but he knows what that is which he can do, nor does he know until he has tried.
> Trust thyself; every heart vibrates to that iron string. Accept the place the Devine Providence has found for you, the society of your contemporaries, the connection of events. Great men have always done so.
> What I must do is all that concerns me, not what people think. This rule, equally arduous in actual and in intellectual life, may serve for the whole distinction between greatness and meanness.

It is the harder because you will always find those who think they know what is your duty better than you know it. It is easy in the world to live after the world's opinion; it is easy in solitude to live after your own; but the great man is he who in the midst of the crowd keeps with perfect sweetness the independence of solitude.

For better or worse, you must cultivate, plant, and water your own garden in your own individual way and your harvest will be in direct proportion to the things that you have done the right way. Always insist on being yourself and never imitate anyone. Nothing can be compared to self-reliance. Don't sacrifice that to anything else.

YOUR UNLIMITED POWER

It's Not What I Think That's Important, It's What You Think

Hundreds of people have asked me, "Do you really think that I'll be able to stand up in front of a group and think on my feet—not go blank? I get so nervous I just die a million deaths." My answer to their question is: "It's not what I think that counts. I know you have the potential to overcome the obstacles and challenges that keep so many people from speaking in public successfully. It's what *you* think that is important. Is there some good, valid reason why you can't?" People will almost always agree that they have the potential—they just haven't developed it yet. I developed the ability, I've seen hundreds of others develop the ability, and so can you! You have unlimited power to overcome obstacles and challenges.

John Dryden said, "They can conquer who believe they can." I am not suggesting that all you have to do is read this book and you will become one of the country's best platform or television speakers. But I am saying that if you study and practice the "rules of the game" you'll become a quality performer. Remember, failures at speaking are divided into two classes: Those who thought and never did and those who did and never thought.

Far too many men and women sell themselves short and

suffer from feelings of inferiority. Henry Link said, "An inferiority complex is seldom more than senseless timidities that rob us of courage, sap ambition, and sap enterprise." Many people fail to try to conquer new challenges because they lack courage. Many fail to realize that defeat is not the worst of failure. *Not to have tried is the true failure.* When you fully know yourself and the powers that are within you, positive motivation takes over. You'll overcome inferiority and the obstacles and challenges of public speaking. You'll be on your way to becoming a confident and effective public speaker.

HOW TO KEEP STAGE FRIGHT IN PROPER PERSPECTIVE

Understand Audience Fear (Stage Fright)

Most people, regardless of occupation and age, cite public speaking as their greatest fear. Just the thought of making a speech; giving a short prayer before a meeting, luncheon, or banquet; giving a short report or conducting a lecture makes for uneasiness and nervousness. They suffer from "butterflies in the stomach," rapid heart beat, sweaty hands, and rapid breathing. As they get closer to the actual speech time, they have thoughts of failing, of no one being interested in what they are going to say, of making a bad scene, or of making mistakes. They are afraid that they will forget part of the talk, or that their minds will go blank, or that their voices will crack and their hands will tremble. If you experience those symptoms, you are not abnormal.

I have had ministers tell me they can get only fifteen or twenty people out of their membership of maybe 300 to 500 to take on leadership responsibilities that require speaking in front of people. I've had officers of various companies, community service clubs, trade associations, PTAs, and professional groups tell me the same thing. By far, the majority of men and women of all ages and professions dislike expressing themselves in a group situation. *So if you have stage fright, you are not alone.*

What causes stage fright? Simply not knowing your

capabilities, or a lack of experience and self-confidence. The more successful speaking experiences you have, the better control of stage fright you have. You'll probably always have some fear, tension, and stress just before you begin a speech, but a few seconds after you get started, those symptoms will vanish.

Dorothy Fosdick said, "Fear is a basic emotion, part of our native equipment, and like all normal emotions has a positive function to perform. Comforting formulas for getting rid of anxiety may be just the wrong thing. Books about 'peace of mind' can be bad medicine. To be afraid when one should be afraid is good sense." Cicero said that all public speaking of real merit was characterized by nervousness. Good speakers want to be their very best and fulfill their responsibilities, even to very small groups; therefore, they meet the stress of the occasion by being excited and keyed up.

Having stage fright shows that you are concerned, that you want to do a good job of meeting the challenge before you, that you care about the outcome of an event, and that you want to be your very best.

Think about this seriously and logically: Why would you want to lose all of something that is your body's way of helping you get ready to do an outstanding job of meeting an unusual challenge?

Recently, I spoke at a convention in Florida. Another speaker and I were visiting during the luncheon break. He told me that he never had any audience fear and that he felt that he was over and above that kind of kindergarten stuff. He said, "The audience doesn't bother me at all. I tell it the way I see it. If the audience likes it, fine; and if they don't, fine." What an attitude! I made it a point to attend his part of the program to see what kind of a job he would do. He was scheduled to speak for twenty minutes, but he quit at the end of fifteen minutes, thank goodness. After he had finished, one conventioneer remarked, "The same old malarky, dry as a bone, delivered by a pompous, overbearing speaker . . . a real dud."

For the most part, I've found that those speakers who say they are always *completely calm* and *tranquil* before they start to speak almost never provide an audience with true inspiration and motivation.

Freeing yourself from negative bondage by controlling fear is an extraordinarily delightful experience. Sell yourself right now on the idea that controlled fear is good. I have talked to many professional speakers and it is agreed that the professionals, like anyone else, have a certain amount of stage fright just before they begin. *They never lose it*—and *they don't want to.* Why? Because they know that controlled stage fright keys them up, gets them ready for action, gets them more spirited and animated. They know that fear gets them ready for action to meet the immediate challenge. They think faster and keener, and they are even more inspirational and motivational because of controlled fear. They speak with even more conviction and intensity because controlled fear helped to get their minds, hearts, and bodies ready for positive action. The experience of controlling fear is extraordinarily delightful. *The professional speaker needs stage fright; the amateur is overwhelmed by it.*

"Nervousness is the price you pay for being a race horse instead of a truck horse," said Professor Ormond Drake. No one has ever gone to the horse races and ever bet on a truck horse beating a race horse. Have you ever watched racehorses as they are being put in the starting gate of the actual race? They are not standing still waiting for something to happen. They are nervous, hard to control and hold down, they are spirited and can hardly wait to jump out of the starting gate the second it is opened. That's the way it is with good speakers. Controlled stage fright has gotten them keyed up and ready to jump into action!

Several years ago, I took my children to the horseraces. I will never forget one incident that occurred that afternoon. We went down to the stalls where they were getting the horses ready for the next race. One of my boys spotted a winner. He called me down to the stall to look at his choice for the next race. He said, "Dad, see what I mean . . . this horse is so nervous, keyed up, and ready for action that they can't hold him down to get the saddle and the jockey on him."

Sure enough, that horse came in first place. There were no truck or work horses that could keep up with that racehorse even for just a few seconds.

YOU MUST HAVE A BURNING DESIRE TO
SUCCEED AT SPEAKING

Wishful Thinking Won't Do

Thus far, I have assured you that you are not abnormal if you have stage fright, excessive audience fear, and that you can free yourself from this negative bondage by learning how to control it. I have also told you that once audience fear is controlled, it is good. You'll never eliminate it, but you certainly can reduce it, adjust to it, speak in spite of it, and even make it work for you. Frank Bettger said, "Don't attempt to lose your nervousness! Use it! Make it work for you!"

You have the potential of accomplishing exactly the goal you want to achieve, provided you want to do it badly enough. Wishful thinking won't do. Wishful thinking by itself is without any positive effect simply because your true inner power factors of real desire, a positive attitude, preparation, and practice are missing.

HOW TO USE YOUR IMAGINATION

Have a Strong, Positive Attitude

Frederick William Robertson said, "To believe is to be strong. Doubt cramps energy. Belief is power." You must not doubt in your heart. You must not allow any negative thoughts and images to exist in your mind. Mark 11:23 tells us, "Whosoever shall say unto this mountain, be thou removed, and be thou cast into the sea; and shall not doubt in his heart, but shall believe that those things which he saith shall come to pass; he shall have whatsoever he saith." With belief in yourself, a positive attitude, a burning desire, a good self-image, plus preparation and practice, you can achieve your speaking goals.

Every accomplishment was first a picture in someone's imagination. Immediately rid yourself of any negative thinking and any negative mind pictures you hold of yourself. Replace them at once with powerful, positive mind pictures in which you see yourself succeeding. Think about the goals you set back in Chapter 1. The more visual you make your goals, the easier it will be for you to visualize your plan of action. Visualize step by step the things that must be done successfully. There's only one way to eat an elephant, and that is one bite at a time. The same is true in accomplishing your speaking goals—do one thing at a time. There is very little, if any, hope for the person who wishes for a "change for the better" if that person cannot accept the right attitude toward the steps that must be taken to bring about that accomplishment.

If you can visualize the successful results of making your objective become a reality and let no negative thoughts crowd out this positive image, with perseverance your dynamic inner powers and action will bring about the successful completion of your speaking goals.

Dr. Maxwell Maltz, author of *The Magic of Self-Image Psychology* (Englewood Cliffs, N.J.: Prentice-Hall, Inc., 1964), tells us how important our self-image really is. Read and study his findings in depth.

> The self-image we harbor is the key to the success or failure of our most cherished plans and aspirations. If the image is inadequate, and psychologists say most of us habitually underrate ourselves, it behooves us to correct it. We do this by systematically imagining that we are already the sort of person we wish to be. If you have been painfully shy, imagine yourself moving among people with ease and poise. If you have been fearful and overanxious, see yourself acting calmly, confidently and with courage.
>
> If we picture ourselves performing in a certain manner, this imaginative exercise impresses our subconscious almost as much as does the actual performance.
>
> Each of us has a mental picture of himself or herself, a self-image which governs much of his or her conduct and outlook. To find life reasonably satisfying you must have a self-image you can live with. You must find yourself acceptable to you. You must have a self that you like, and one that you can trust and believe in. When this self-image is one you can be proud of, you feel self-confident. You function at your best.

Use your imagination to form positive mental images in which you see yourself succeeding in every one of your endeavors.

HOW TO DESTROY NEGATIVE THOUGHTS

To Feel Brave, Act As If You Are Brave

Just as our positive mental attitude and images are important, it's also important to act the successful person you see in you mind. Professor William James of Harvard said this about action and feeling:

> Action seems to follow feeling, but really action and feeling go together; and by regulating the action, which is under the more direct control of the will, we can indirectly regulate the feeling which is not. Thus the sovereign voluntary path to cheerfulness, if our spontaneous cheerfulness be lost, is to sit up cheerfully and to act and speak as if cheerfulness were already there. If such conduct does not make you feel cheerful, nothing else on that occasion can. So to feel brave, act as if you are brave, use all of your will to that end, and a courage-fit will very likely replace the fit of fear.

Act as if you believe in yourself, and you will have the *feeling* you believe in yourself.

I encourage you to start immediately using James' advice. To develop courage and confidence when you are speaking to an audience, act like the courageous and confident speaker you desire to be. Soon the feeling will be there. *Feelings follow actions.*

Dorothea Brande said, "Act as if it were impossible to fail." This means that you must act confidently. Make those few words part of your nervous system. Repeat them frequently. Remember, fear is nothing more than lack of self-confidence, and lack of self-confidence comes from lack of experience. The more successful experiences you have, the more self-confidence you will gain and the better control of fear and stage fright you will have.

I assure you that you will appear more confident before a group than you feel on the inside. I also can assure you that if you deliver your speeches with desire, determination, and dedication, along with all the ideas and techniques discussed throughout this chapter and the entire book, your fear of audience rejection or fear of failure just will not come about.

In speaking, just as it is with anything in life, it's the *getting started* that's difficult, but don't procrastinate. Webster defines *procrastinate* as, "to put off doing (something unpleasant or burdensome) until a future time, to postpone (such actions) habitually." It's only natural that the first few times we do anything new and strange to us we are going to feel fearful and have some self-doubt. Remember this: *If you can do a thing once, you can do it twice. If you can do it twice, you can do it three times. If you can do it three times, you can make a habit of it.* Trust me and believe me. From my experience, I know you will do better than you think you will, and each time it will get a little easier. You'll soon be making a habit of doing the right things in the right way for you to ensure your success.

HOW TO TURN KNOWLEDGE INTO ABILITY

Acquire Ability by Practicing and Actually Speaking

Some of you don't want to become professional public speakers. You just want to be able to get up, think on your feet, and say clearly what's on your mind when they ask for "any suggestions from the membership." Some of you want to take a more active role in your church work, PTA, clubs, and organizational work. Others may want to become more professional at speaking at company meetings, making presentations in the board room, or handling public relations assignments. Others may want to become professionals to speak at conventions, conferences, and large gatherings. Regardless of your goal, the ideas and techniques discussed in this book are as important to one kind of speaker as they are to the other kind. I will supply the knowledge. What I can't supply for you is the practice and the experience you will gain from actually speaking in public. The only way to develop the ability to be a confident and influential speaker is to speak! *Principles must be practiced and repeated until you are complete master of them.* Every time the principles are put into practice and repeated, you will grow stronger and feel more confident and in control of your situation.

Learning to fly an airplane is very similar. First you go to school to get the necessary knowledge. Before you can become a qualified pilot, you must practice flying the airplane, first with an instructor and then solo, for a determined number of hours. You must find out how the plane acts and reacts to your various moves and commands when applying your classroom knowledge. All the time, you are feeling more confident because you are practicing putting your knowledge to use in an actual situation. Each flying experience builds more self-confidence. Soon you are a qualified confident pilot. The amateur pilot becomes a skilled or professional pilot by going through the same procedure. That's the way it works in speaking also.

The great orator William Jennings Bryan said, "The ability to speak effectively is an acquirement rather than a gift." And the key to acquiring the ability is through practice and speaking. There are no substitutes or shortcuts.

Don't Let Self-Consciousness Stop You from Practicing

In my thirteen years of teaching public speaking, I made an important discovery. Most people appeared on the outside to be a lot more confident and in control of a situation than they felt on the inside. Speakers were judging their outside appearance by the way they felt on the inside.

I will never forget a student named Gene. When Gene had finished giving his first speech, I congratulated him on the fine, confident way he handled himself. His reply was: "I'm like a swan swimming across a lake. I look calm and confident on the part you can see above the water, but boy are those feet busy kicking under the surface of the water."

Gene was acting confident in spite of his inner nervousness and the butterflies in his stomach. His progress was remarkable. He went at speaking just the way a cat goes after a bird in a bird cage . . . he knew what he wanted and in earnest. After several speeches, his stage fright could be compared to most good speakers. He had some nervousness or self-consciousness just before he started, but after he was a few seconds into his talk, it quickly disappeared. His experience can be your experience also.

HOW TO KEEP MISTAKES IN PROPER FOCUS

Don't Be Discouraged by Mistakes

By having the right attitude, being properly organized and prepared and having practiced your talk, you virtually have eliminated the possibilities of big mistakes. I mention this because many, many people are so self-conscious that they won't even try to practice speaking. They are too afraid of making a mistake. *The person who is afraid to make mistakes is afraid to succeed.* Ralph Waldo Emerson said, "Every mistake is an opportunity for learning." As long as we learn something from a mistake, we are making every experience a successful experience. Each mistake is bringing you a little bit closer to your goal accomplishment. You are human, and every once in a while you may make a small error. You must be willing to accept a mistake now and then.

When you are doing something that you've never done before, no matter how poorly it turns out, you're on your way to doing it better next time. Whatever error you might have made, you are much further along toward your goal achievement than if you had never attempted to do it at all. *It's the person who doesn't try who guarantees his or her failure.* Whenever you make a mistake, ask yourself, "What did I learn from that experience?" Mistakes are opportunities to learn, and each one gets you closer to where you really want to be.

Don't Be a Member of the "What If I . . ." Club

Here are some common "What-if-I" phrases that I frequently hear:

"What if I don't gesture properly ..."
"What if I don't communicate right ..."
"What if I do something to make the audience laugh at me ..."
"What if I go completely blank from a mental block ..."
"What if I don't look at the audience right ..."
"What if I forget to ..."
"What if I make a mistake ..."
and "What if I fumble a word or phrase ..."

You should be concerned about doing your very best and holding errors to a minimum. That's the type of person you are or you wouldn't be reading this book. However, don't be so overly concerned that it blocks your progress. First, as you master the various speaking techniques outlined in this book, you are reducing your chances of error. Second, really embarrassing mistakes very seldom happen. Stop and think, when was the last time you saw one occur? You'll have to think for a long time to come up with just one incident that was really serious. So the odds are against anything like that happening to you. Third, audiences are forgiving. No audience has ever shot a speaker for making a minor error or fumbling a word or phrase. Every one of us makes small, insignificant errors in everyday conversation with another person. Fumbling a word or phrase will happen to the best of speakers once in a while. The audience understands this. In fact, you can turn an error into your advantage by using a little humor, laughing about it, and keeping calm. When you have fumbled a word or phrase, try some of these simple one-liners that speakers use to smooth over a minor error.

"I just paid $500.00 to get my eyes fixed and now my mouth won't work."
"My pep pills are running way ahead of my tranquilizers."
"I had a clinker in my thinker."
"Let me try that again—only this time in English."
"My wife (or husband) told me not to buy my partial (or teeth) at the hardware store."

The consequences of making a mistake are exaggerated in our minds. Being overly concerned about fumbles stems from fear. As you get more successful speaking experiences behind you, fear and being overly concerned about mistakes will disappear.

TEN WAYS TO CREATE SPEAKING OPPORTUNITIES

Good Speakers Are in Demand

You may be saying to yourself, "After I get my speech organized, prepared, and have practiced it, where can I go to actually give my talk so that I can continue to grow by the experience of actually speaking?" Lowell Thomas said, "Leadership gravitates to the person who can talk." Good speakers are in demand. The word gets around very quickly about good speakers (and bad ones, too!). Here then are some ideas about where you can create opportunities to give your talks to grow as a speaker.

1. Join a speaking group like Toastmasters or Toastmistresses. This is an excellent choice for anyone who wants to grow and stay sharp. The members help each other become more efficient and effective speakers. You have an opportunity to grow not only as a speaker, but you'll learn a great deal by evaluating other speakers.

2. Call your church and tell the minister or an assistant that you would like to join a certain group, and then take an active part in the discussions and various project work. Volunteer to help out a a committee chairperson, or perhaps become a counselor for a youth group or teach a Sunday School class. You'll have many opportunities to give progress reports and all kinds of talks before groups.

3. Join a service club or fraternal or professional group. Volunteer to head up a committee and give various committee reports or become the program chairman so you can introduce the speaker each week or month. If you are really active in the group, you'll have many opportunities to express yourself before the group.

4. Attend various government meetings such as city council, public utilities special meetings, the homeowners' association, school meetings, special project taxation meetings, or planning and zoning commission meetings. There are many meetings such as these every week. Stand up and speak up on key issues. It's an

excellent way to develop your ability to get your point across briefly and effectively.

5. Stand up and contribute ideas at your company or corporate meetings. You are bound to have ideas that management is looking for.

6. Offer to present a worthwhile program at your next convention, annual meeting, sales and management conference, or at the board meeting.

7. Volunteer to head up a group of boy scouts; girl scouts; summer youth camps; Little League softball, football, baseball, basketball, soccer; or a 4-H group. There are many more.

8. Join a self-help group such as financial planning, gardening, Bible study, business person's breakfast, or a sales and management club.

9. Join a business or trade association, chamber of commerce, political organization, or hobby group and speak out with your constructive ideas.

10. Develop two or three effective, informative, and/or entertaining talks and call various groups and offer to be the program at one of their meetings. If you're good, your phone will ring constantly. You'll be in demand.

I could go on, but when you are serious about looking for places to give your speeches in public, you will find more opportunities than you have time for. If you are good, you'll be a much sought-after person, because those who can speak effectively stand head and shoulders above those people who don't and won't. All the time, you will be gaining additional courage and experience, and you'll be growing and developing into a dynamic, confident public speaker and leader.

THE MORE URGENT YOUR TRUE DESIRE, THE FASTER YOU WILL PROGRESS

You Can Overcome Any Obstacle That May Stand in Your Way

Be yourself and believe in yourself. Get excited about yourself. *You've got everything it takes to get what you genuinely want!!*

You must truly know and understand yourself. Your progress toward becoming a confident and effective public speaker is in your hands. No one can do it for you. The more urgent your heartfelt desire, the faster your progress. See yourself in your positive mind pictures achieving your goals, step by step. Your inner motivating forces make the difference between failing at speaking or succeeding at speaking, between being a stock clerk or an executive or between being a nobody or a professional person. Practice every principle in this book until it becomes a habit.

The One Thing Most Successful People Have in Common

After observing and training men and women from all walks of life in speech, sales, management, and communications seminars, I have come to this conclusion: Successful people *know themselves.* They develop their potential and their own style to the fullest. Well over ninety-percent of them are confident and effective public speakers. They are able to express themselves in such a way that they are clearly understood and their ideas are acted upon. Their individual way of getting things accomplished and of presenting their ideas has brought them important recognition, a promotion, a larger paycheck, or has added more profit to the business. All of them enjoy the self-satisfaction of knowing that they, in their own unique way, have contributed to the success of many community, business, church, and school functions.

Know yourself and don't let anything or anybody stop you from developing your potential to the fullest in your own individual way. *You've got what it takes to get what you want.*

"GARDLINES"

1. The triangle of successful speaking consists of: *Know Yourself, Know Your Speech,* and *Know Your Audience.*
2. Don't try to imitate others. You must be you. Develop your own style.
3. You have personal characteristics that no one else has. Use them to the fullest.

4. You have unlimited power to overcome obstacles and challenges.
5. It's not what I think that's important. It's what you think that counts.
6. Free yourself from negative bondage.
7. Most people cite public speaking as their greatest fear. If you have audience fear, you are not abnormal.
8. Do not allow stage fright to control you. You control it.
9. The professional speaker needs stage fright while the amateur is overwhelmed by it.
10. You must have a burning desire to succeed at speaking.
11. Use your imagination to form positive mental images.
12. To feel brave, act as if you are brave.
13. Act confident. Feelings follow actions.
14. Go at every speech with desire, determination, and dedication.
15. Knowledge becomes ability through practice.
16. The ability to speak effectively is an acquirement rather than a gift.
17. The person who is afraid to make mistakes is afraid to succeed.
18. Each mistake brings you closer to your goal accomplishment.
19. You can create many places to speak—it's opportunity unlimited.
20. The more urgent your desire, the faster you will progress.
21. Your inner motivating forces make the difference between failing at speaking or succeeding at speaking.
22. When you really know yourself, you know you've got what it takes to get what you want.

THOUGHT-PROVOKING QUOTES

Putting off an easy thing makes it difficult, putting off a hard one makes it impossible.
GEORGE H. LORIMER

The faster you go, the more chance of stubbing your toe, but the more chance you have of getting somewhere.
CHARLES F. KETTERING

My duty as an intellectual is to think, to think without restriction, even at the risk of blundering. I must set no limits within myself, and I must let no limits be set for me.
JEAN-PAUL SARTRE

What the superior man seeks is in him; what

the common man seeks
is in others.
CONFUCIUS

Work is the best method
devised for killing time.
WILLIAM FEATHER

Man is not the creature of
circumstances; circumstances
are the creatures of man.
BENJAMIN DISRAELI

A man's doubts and fears
are his worst enemies.
WILLIAM WRIGLEY JR.

It is the character of a
brave and resolute man not
to be ruffled by adversity
and not to desert his post.
CICERO

What we think, or what we
know, or what we believe
is, in the end, of little
consequence. The only
consequence is what we do.
JOHN RUSKIN

After a man makes his mark
in the world, a lot of people

will come around with erasers.
FRANK G. McINNIS

Things cannot always go your
way. Learn to accept in silence
the minor aggravations,
cultivate
the gift of taciturnity and
consume your own smoke with
an extra draught of hard
work,
so that those about you may
not be annoyed with the dust
and soot of your complaints.
WILLIAM OSLER

To know one's self is,
above all, to know what
one lacks. It is to measure
one's self against truth,
and not the other way around.
FLANNERY O'CONNOR

Optimism is a kind of heart
stimulus—the digitalis
of failure.
ELBERT HUBBARD

To be good, a man must
do something every day
to help himself.
PAUL BRYANT

4

KNOW YOUR AUDIENCE

The one completely unforgivable
fault in speaking is to neglect the audience.

WEAVER

Capture the Audience

HOW TO CAPTURE AND HOLD YOUR AUDIENCE'S ATTENTION

Speak the Audience's Language

"This speaker knows who we are" or "This speaker is talking our language and really knows us": These are the words you must have the audience saying to themselves immediately when your *start* your speech or you will end up talking to yourself. Arthur C. Fuller said, "You must have a pleasant manner and be able to make a favorable impression in thirty seconds." Audiences react fast and are quick to judge if you are a speaker worth listening to, if you can identify with them, if you are sincerely interested in them, and if you want to get your message across. *The audience will be interested in you only after you have shown honest and sincere interest in them.* The key is to make a complete analysis of your listeners.

Regardless of your topic, bring in one or two remarks at the beginning of your speech that are *pertinent and directly targeted to your specific audience.* It's always good to tell them something that they didn't think you would know about them as a group or to mention the names of one or two people who are in the audience and why the group should be proud of them. Congratulations are always in order for some special achievement that the group has accomplished. Perhaps you can identify with a particular current problem or situation that's bound to be on the listeners' minds. Be brief, honest, and sincere. This technique helps you to ensure a receptive, appreciative, and responsive audience.

Before you accept an invitation to speak, you should know *exactly* the type of people who will make up the audience and *exactly* what impact the meeting planner wants your talk to make on the listeners. Finding out this critical information a few minutes before you speak or trying to size up the group after you have started speaking is too late. I know of no speaker who could go before an audience and feel confident and comfortable unless he or she knows who is in the audience and can speak the audience's language. I would rather go before an audience stark naked than to be unfamiliar with the type of people I would be addressing. A few well-worded questions and a few minutes of time will help you to make an accurate analysis of your listeners.

Be Flexible

It is important that you give the *right talk* to the *right audience*. Even though your expertise and topic would fit almost any group, it's always a good idea to personalize at least two or three points of your talk. Audiences love that tailored and personal touch! This may make you doubtful that you can and should speak to certain groups. Naturally, if you feel you are uncomfortable speaking to a certain group, by all means do not accept the engagement. Be honest with the person who extended the invitation to you. State that you do not feel qualified to speak to his or her group. Your honesty will be admired. The last thing the meeting planner and the audience want is a "bummer" or "failure" on their hands. That's also the last thing you want.

However, it's very surprising and enlightening when you ask in-depth questions about a group. You'll find several areas in which, if you are flexible and creative, you can tailor your material to make it applicable to an audience's specific situation. We see this happening every day. For example, professional football players and coaches address many audiences each year; they tell salespeople, for instance, how to use the same winning attitude and determination in their profession to increase their sales as is used on the football field. A football player's winning attitude can help anyone, regardless of his or her education or occupation, to reach his or her personal or professional goals. The topic of a winning attitude, with flexible tailoring, could be presented to any type of group.

Naturally, depending on the speech purpose and topic, many talks on a variety of subjects and for diverse purposes can be given with little or no tailoring for the specific group. However, to be even more successful and to build maximum audience rapport, it still would be important to identify with the group. This is why you must not only know the audience, but you must know exactly the impact the meeting planner wants made. A key guideline for speaking success is—*deliver your talk with a personalized flavor.*

Don't ever lose sight of the fact that the audience is made up of many people just like you with emotions and feelings. Always respect them and sincerely care about them. *Never think of your listeners as being "living, breathing backboards" for the words of your speech.*

In-depth questioning involves a lot of hard work, but I believe that any confident and influential speaker will tell you that effective speaking is hard work. To be successful at anything requires hard work and making sure that you are doing the right things right. For sure, one of the right things to do when speaking in public is knowing your audience well and knowing the expected specific impact of your speech on that particular group of people. It's the difference between a mediocre talk (or failure) and a highly successful talk, between reaching the audience or sitting down frustrated knowing that you didn't get through to the group.

Nothing Can Come Out of a Speaker That Is Not Already Inside the Speaker

If a speaker isn't willing to work hard to find out vital background information about his or her audience and tailor the message for the specific group to create the right impact, he or she should not accept the engagement. *You win an audience by persuasion, not by force.* To be persuasive with a particular group, you must have audience knowledge on the inside. What a speaker has on the inside shows up very clearly on the outside. If you won't look good doing it, don't do it! If you don't fully respect your audience, don't give the talk. The audience won't respect you, and rightly so. Theodore Roosevelt said, "I am only an average man but, by George, I work harder at it than the average man."

Speaking to an audience can be compared to looking into a mirror. If we look in the mirror and we are smiling, those smiles are returned. The audience reaction to a speaker is a reflection just like a mirror.

HOW TO EARN THE AUDIENCE'S LOYALTY

You Cannot Beg, Borrow, or Steal Audience Loyalty

You must earn it. Every move you make, every word you speak, and every feeling you have must communicate to the audience that you respect them, like them, trust them, and admire them. You'll get back from an audience exactly what you have sent to them, no more or less. Sincerely let the audience know that you appreciate them and that they are important. William James of Harvard said, "The deepest principle in human nature is the craving to be appreciated." The majority always rules. Thus, when you have fulfilled the deepest craving and desire of the majority of the people in your audience, you have created a positive atmosphere for you and your speech. A positive atmosphere paves the way for earning audience loyalty.

FIFTEEN CRITICAL KEYS TO CREATE YOUR POSITIVE ACCEPTANCE

The Amateurs Take These Points Lightly
While Professionals Take Them Seriously

The professionals in any field know all the things that must be done to ensure success. *That's why professionals make difficult things look simple and easy.* Don't skip over these points lightly. They are all very important in successfully getting your point across to a group.

1. *What is the exact purpose of the meeting?* Is this a weekly, monthly, semiannual, or annual meeting? Is it a special meeting? Has the meeting been called because of a crisis situation, or is it a regular business meeting? Will you be the only speaker on the program, or will there be other speakers? If so, what are their topics? Will new products or concepts be presented? Will prize winners be announced and awards presented? If so, for what?

It's vital to find out if some of the audience will be upset or displeased because of some event that has occurred or is about to occur. Will the audience be happy because of an announcement to be made? What projects does the organization sponsor? Is this an organizational meeting for the annual fundraising project? Although it is a regular meeting, you should be fully aware of any special situations such as elections, special music or singing, or voting issues that are coming up at the meeting.

To illustrate the importance of these various points, I am going to cite feedback comments for you from various places where I have spoken. I do this to help you understand what meeting planners are looking for in speakers. "Your outstanding presentation was very meaningful and appropriate for the current conditions in agriculture. Your positive, inspirational talk was a speciality at our 50th anniversary meeting," and "This was the first time to bring all segments of the industry together and it was important that things went right. Your comments and manner of presentation did the trick." Feedback from another planner said, "We were especially happy in the way you were able to adjust and structure your talk to our current situation and future plans." I cannot stress too strongly the importance of knowing why the group is assembling. Before you can compose a speech, it is imperative that you know the exact purpose of the meeting.

2. *What is the theme of the meeting?* Mention the theme two or three times (don't over do it) in your talk and make a few relative comments about it. As a speaker, you can reinforce the program chairperson's theme. Both the program chairperson and the audience will appreciate it. After all, it's important to everyone present or it wouldn't have been selected.

Here's a couple of feedback comments from meeting planners: "You set the stage, followed our convention theme in your remarks, and did an outstanding job with your keynote address," and "We appreciate the manner in which you helped to develop our overall meeting theme."

Knowing the meeting theme and mentioning it two or three times is an excellent way to personalize your talk.

3. *What are the occupations of the listeners?* Is the group made up of household executives, farmer, engineers, professional secretaries, students, school teachers, customers, parents, businesspeople, employees, engineers, doctors, lawyers, or ex-

ecutives? How long have they been in this occupation? Are they old-timers or new on the job? Will their spouses be present? Some audiences are composed of people with a wide variety of backgrounds and occupations, but if you dig deeply you'll find some common interests. You may be requested to make some specific remarks directed toward a specific group in the audience. The meeting planner may want you to do this. In that case, he should advise the audience in the introduction that he has requested you to talk directly to the (X) group. One meeting planner, who asked me to talk to his sales personnel and not to his production management people who were also present, wrote, "Your talk was 'on the money' in that it applied to sales personnel directly."

A request like that does not happen very often. Most of the time, the meeting planner wants you to include everyone in the audience. Unless you have been specifically requested to ignore a certain group in the audience, build your talk in such a way that all attendees feel you have something to say to them. Somehow, some way, include all occupations and attendees in your talk or you'll lose the audience. One program chairman wrote, "With the variety of people attending, we know it was not easy to tailor a presentation to our group. Your ability to deliver a thoughtful message with humor that everyone enjoyed was outstanding."

It will take a lot of thought and work to tailor your talk to include the whole audience, but it can be done. *Speak to all occupations in the audience unless the meeting planner has requested you to speak to a particular segment of the group.*

4. *What have the listeners been exposed to and what was their attitude toward the subject and toward the speaker?* Who spoke last week, month, or year? What was the specific subject? What was the reaction? If it was well received, why? If it was not well received, why?

This valuable information will help you in preparing your speech for your audience. If the speaker or the subject "bombed" at the last meeting and you know *why*, you can prosper from someone else's experience and make yourself look good by preparing a more effective, successful speech.

When a meeting planner who advised me that last year's speaker flopped, I found out *why*. Therefore, I felt very comfortable both in preparing and delivering my talk. The planner wrote, "You surely sensed that your comments were well received. It was just what the doctor ordered! Thanks for fitting in so well and for a masterful job." The meeting planner had told me everything I needed to know about my audience to ensure success.

If you have any doubts about how the listeners will receive the subject that the meeting planner has requested you to speak on, ask him or her about the probable attitude of the audience. It's only fair to the speaker to know this in advance. If you have been asked to speak on a controversial topic, you will need time to prepare a diplomatic and skillful talk to avoid negative response. Information about the probable attitude of the audience will tell the speaker not to get upset when the audience response is not up to par. *Sometimes the program chairperson will ask the speaker to talk on a subject that the audience won't like to hear, but one which he or she feels should be heard.*

For example, I was asked to speak to a group in an industry that had been hard hit by poor economic times. Their morale was very low. I verified this with the meeting planner when I accepted the engagement. I worked hard in preparing this talk, because I knew that the audience could completely ignore me or could even get up and walk out. I've never had this happen and I didn't want this to be the first time. While everyone kept their seats, audience response was minimal and disappointing. Ten days later, the feedback I received from the meeting planner read, "A true yardstick of an excellent presentation is positive comments days later. Our staff received numerous compliments regarding your enthusiastic talk. Days later, they realized that you skillfully disguised a message that really hit home. An excellent presentation."

Recently, I delivered a luncheon speech to a trade association in Kansas City. The morning general session closing speaker was requested to talk on a subject that was received very negatively by the audience. During the luncheon that followed, one of the attendees told me, "While we didn't like the speaker and his views, we still respect him because he told us the truth in many areas where we have been doing things wrong!"

Knowing your audience's attitude is extremely important in proper preparation and delivery of your speech.

5. *What is the overall income range of the audience?* You are certainly going to address a group in the $75,000-a-year income bracket much differently than a group in the $15,000 income bracket. Program planners know their people, and it's not out of line for you to ask them the income level of those you'll be addressing. Is this group made up of volunteer workers or are they paid workers? Are the attendees paid on an incentive commission arrangement or are they paid a straight salary?

One feedback letter stated, "Although talking to a sophisticated, experienced group of personnel and industrial relations managers, you developed a degree of enthusiasm in your audience that was beyond our expectations." This was a high-income-level group. The income level of the group will give you many clues as to how you should prepare and deliver your speech.

6. *What is the educational background of the group?* Are they college graduates, high school graduates, or dropouts? Are they Ph.D.s? Have some of the listeners been presented outstanding awards because of their work in certain fields or because of important research work they have done? Has the meeting planner asked you to speak as the opener for an intense training school, or have you been asked to be the wrap-up for a two- to four-week intense specialized training program that the group has just completed?

One feedback letter stated, "The way you were able to 'weave' our philosophy into your comments was very impressive, a job well done." Again, I mention these feedback letters to let you know the tremendous importance that meeting planners place on your knowing your audience.

7. *What is the age of the audience?* If you are talking to people in their sixties and seventies, you surely want to speak in language and terms with which they can identify. On the other hand, when speaking to a group of teenagers or people in their twenties, speak in terms and language with which they would

identify. Expressions that would appeal to the senior group may leave the younger group "cold." People in their thirties and forties are far more interested in subjects and events that apply to their age group than would apply to the other age groups. If you are addressing a mixed age group, you must prepare your talk so that it will be interesting to all ages in your audience.

A youth group wrote to tell me, "We felt your presentation was an excellent way to start off the Youth Institute week as you generated so much enthusiasm in delegates."

8. *Is the group male, female, or both?* There are more and more women in the business and professional world today than ever before. There are also more men employed in traditionally female fields. I'm sure most professionals would tell you there is very little, if any, difference in speaking to a group of female executives versus male executives, female employees versus male employees, female organizations versus male organizations. Why should there be? It is important that you speak to men and women as equals and that you do not differentiate between them or talk down to either sex.

Speakers must update and modernize their terminology and phraseology. Instead of saying "businessmen," speakers should use "businesspeople." Instead of saying "chairman," speakers should use "chairperson." It is mandatory that speakers use the correct, updated terminology and expressions that cover both men and women. Most groups today are "mixed" listeners and you would naturally speak to them just like you would to single-sex groups or visa versa. Use terms and expressions that cover both men and women.

9. *How many people will be in the audience?* It is vital to know how many listeners are going to be in the audience. With fifteen or twenty, you would certainly be able to get by without a microphone and your delivery could be more informal. If needed, a chalkboard or flip chart would suffice. With 300 listeners in your audience, you naturally would use a microphone so that you can be clearly heard, your delivery would be more formal, and you would use some type of projector or visual aid that all can see clearly. A chalkboard or flip chart would not be readable to everyone in the audience. Thus, while your

message would be the same, different size groups call for different preparation and a different style of delivery. Since the size of the audience ties in closely with the actual meeting room, the balance of my remarks concerning the size of the audience will be included in the next category.

10. *Where will the meeting be held?* Will the meeting be held in the plant conference room, the church basement, a meeting room in a motel/hotel, the civic auditorium, the American Legion hall, the college cafeteria, or the ballroom off the lounge in the Country Club? *Putting the wrong size group in the wrong room and/or a poor seating arrangement can kill an audience.* The wrong size group or one seated the wrong way can be a complete disaster, even if the meeting is held in a beautiful room. Knowing the physical conditions where you will speak to your group is part of knowing your audience, because an audience will respond differently in different types of room set-ups. Many times a speaker has no control over selecting the right meeting room, but do try to request as many of these things as you feel you can.

Ideally, the room should be just large enough for the group and no larger, with doors that close so that nothing distracts the audience such as onlookers peeking in and hall noise. The room should be quiet so that no bands, speakers, music, projectors, or P.A. noise can be heard from the room next door.

Ask the meeting planner for a complete description of the facility at which you will be speaking, so you will know how the audience will be seated. Some speakers will send the meeting planner a diagram showing how they would prefer the room to be set up in order to get maximum results. *Do not take the size of the room and the seating arrangement lightly.* A scattered audience in a much larger than necessary room can and probably will kill the speaker and his or her message. Unfortunately, many meeting planners and hotel/motel room set-up personnel are not aware of this. A firm guideline to follow is: *All audiences, small or large, must be kept as compact as possible and as close to the speaker as possible.*

Recently, I delivered a keynote luncheon speech in Florida. Right after breakfast, I contacted the hotel room set-up supervisor and the company meeting planner and reconfirmed the way I wanted the room to be set up. The room was too large for the group. I had no control over that. It was the only room available. The next best thing I could do would be to have the attendees compact and as close to me as possible. Even though I drew a diagram of the way I wanted the room to be set up and both people said they understood, at 10 A.M. when I went back to check on the room, what I found was unbelievable. This was a buffet luncheon. Of all things, the food buffet was set up right in the middle of the room with the tables scattered on both sides, spread out all over the room with vast amounts of space between each table and the buffet set-up. In addition to the room being too large, the audience was now divided into two separate groups! While I was not able to get them to a rearrange the buffet line, I did get them to rearrange and make the tables as compact as possible, making the best out of a bad situation. The talk did prove successful, but it could have been even more so had the audience not been split into two groups.

Once I spoke to about 200 people who were scattered in a university auditorium that holds about 7,500. There was a ground level and two balcony levels. I asked the meeting planner to have someone direct the audience into the chairs directly in front of me, making the group as compact as possible. The meeting planner refused (only because he didn't realize the importance of my request), and the 200 people were scattered over three levels. Some were so far away from me that I could barely see their outlines. I used every ounce of energy in me and every speaking technique I know of trying to reach the audience. While the audience heard the basic message, there was no group enthusiasm, inspiration, and motivation. I was trapped in a most undesirable set of circumstances, and even though I tried to prevent this situation, I received no cooperation. Unfortunately when this happens it is the speaker who looks bad, not the meeting planner.

Many times, a speaker is asked to speak to a group from a stage, leaving much space between the speaker and the audience. A word of caution worth repeating from the above example is: Beware of the facility in which there is a balcony and the chairs are fastened to the floor. Unless you have a large enough audience to fill all levels completely, make sure the audience is directed to the chairs right in front of you on one level. Remember, people usually will sit in the back of the room or off by themselves, and you do not want this to happen. Rope off an area for people to sit in or have several "helpers" direct people to the right sitting area. It's far better to get people seated correctly as they arrive than it is to ask them to move up after they have been seated. However, if necessary, either you or the program chairman (it's much better if he or she does it) can ask that everyone move forward and closer.

A speaker often has no choice but to work under adverse conditions, but try to do everything possible to make the room and the seating arrangement as right as possible for your success. You want favorable audience acceptance and response and that comes from getting through to your group logically and emotionally. This can best be accomplished after you have made conditions right for your success.

I can tell you from experience that I have spoken to a scattered group in a large meeting room and have gotten very little, if any, audience response. The very next day, using the same speech material, I have spoken to the same-size group seated properly in the proper size room and have gotten excellent audience response. *Wide open spaces and empty chairs will dampen and/or kill the positive impact of your speech.*

A person who is in a compact audience tends to lose his or her individuality because he or she becomes a member of the group. A group is much easier to move then single individuals who are seated all around the room. As a member of a group, a person will accept and respond to things that would leave him or her unmoved as a single individual. It seems as if there's magic in group enthusiasm, inspiration, or motivation.

Unless you find it absolutely essential to stand on a stage or platform, I suggest that you don't do it. *You'll move the group much easier and better if you get down on the same level with them and stand as close to them as possible.* I am very much aware that sometimes this is impossible.

Henry Ward Beecher said, "People often say, 'Do you think it is much more inspiring to speak to a large audience than a small one?' No I say, I can speak just as well to twelve persons as to a thousand, provided those twelve are crowded around me and close together, so that they can touch each other. But even a thousand people with four feet of space between every two of them, would be just the same as an empty room. Crowd your audience together and you will set them off with half the effort."

Here's a technique that works wonders to ensure that you successfully get people seated correctly. If you are expecting 100 people, it is far better to set up 80 chairs. Why? *You head off a problem before it ever exists.* All eighty chairs will be filled before you set up more chairs. There are always a few no-shows. If the other twenty people show up, you can quickly set up more chairs from extras that you had hidden on hand in the back of the room just in case you might need them. This not only lets you have the audience seated right where you want them, but it makes the event look like a bigger success when you have to set up more chairs. Too few people in too many chairs makes the event look like a failure.

In sum, small groups should be placed in small rooms and large groups in large rooms, but regardless of the size of the group, it's far better to pack the aisles and have a full house than to have your listeners scattered with lots of dead space between them. Believe me, what I have said about the size of the meeting room and the seating of the audience is true and important. Do everything you can to prevent a negative experience and to make your speech a positive success. It is vital that you know how the audience will respond in various-size meeting rooms and seating arrangements.

11. *What's on the meeting agenda right before you speak?* What happens right before you speak can affect your audience. If you are following a speaker who "bombed," or one the audience didn't like, or one who spoke on a very controversial subject, he or she can literally kill the audience for you. Be prepared! If that happens, you'll have to work extra hard to get the audience back on track, but they usually can be won back.

I always make it a point to find out *exactly* what is happening before I speak, and even then I have been occasionally misinformed. I caution you again: Be prepared.

For example, I was booked to speak from 9:30 A.M. until 10:30 A.M. at a management meeting in Los Angeles. The meeting was to open at 9:00 A.M. with fifteen minutes for an update message from the company president followed with a fifteen-minute update message from the vice president of operations. I had verified the agenda the night before, including schedule and update highlights that each would give. The meeting opened on time with the president giving his update message. The audience didn't like what they heard, and soon the meeting turned into a "gripe session" with no leadership being shown by the president. The more he talked, the more angry the audience became. The president started at 9:00 A.M. and continued speaking until 10:30 A.M. The vice president of operations cut his talk so that I could give my speech and still have time to catch my plane. You can imagine how the audience immediately responded to me. The president angered the audience, and now they were skeptical of me and my message. I've never seen a more irate group. After about fifteen minutes, I began to win the audience over, and they had warmed up pretty well by the time I was through. My point is, to know your audience you must realize how events prior to your speaking set the tone and affect how you will be received.

As another example, I was to speak at a convention luncheon being held in Lake Tahoe, California. The meeting planner had asked me to give a very enthusiastic and humorous talk containing a positive message. I checked with the meeting planner early that morning to find out exactly what was going to happen at the convention general session that morning, after lunch was eaten, and before I would start speaking. I was assured that a routine business meeting with no special issues would be held in the morning and that I was to speak immediately following lunch.

Well, the meeting planner made other arrangements and didn't tell me about them. He and the association president got together sometime later that morning and decided to hold a ten-minute memorial service for an association member who had recently passed away. The first I knew about it was when the emcee started the program right after lunch. I sat there thinking he was going to introduce me, but instead he started the memorial service. Can you imagine how I felt? There I was, ready to give an enthusiastic, motivational, humorous talk immediately following a very moving, sad memorial service. Thank goodness for presence of mind. I wrote a fast note to the meeting planner and asked him to come on the program immediately after the memorial service and make every convention announcement he could. I suggested that he do anything he could think of to fill two or three minutes of time to give the audience a chance to get their minds back on the convention. It worked! I was able to start off strong and be effective. I never cease to be amazed at how many things like that come up even after I take steps to prevent such events.

If you are following an event or a speaker who went over well, the audience will be warmed up for you. That makes it nice and easy. If you are following a heavy, dry lecture-type presentation, you can quickly win the audience over to you and your style. One meeting planner wrote, "I was not sure that anyone could stimulate a group of 450 people following a heavy diet of rather dry, lecture-type presentations. Your humorous, dynamic delivery lifted everyone's spirits and sent them home with a nice warm feeling about the entire meeting."

If the audience has been left in a neutral, good, or excellent mood and frame of mind by the prior speaker, the audience will have an open mind and be receptive to you. If the audience is in a poor or negative frame of mind because of the previous speaker, you'll have to work hard to reopen their minds and make them receptive. With patience and a well-prepared speech, most of the time it can be done. In some cases, however, the audience may well choose to keep a closed mind. In that case, do three things: first, be patient and understanding; second, keep trying by doing your very best; and third; don't blame yourself.

I am suggesting that you know your audience as of the very minute you are introduced. Knowing your audience lets you know exactly what you must do to win them over immediately.

12. *What is the morale of the group?* When an audience starts arriving, everything each person has seen or heard to that point in his or her life comes with him or her to the inside of the meeting room. An audience is the sum total of the attitudes and

the events that have taken place in each person's life. We live in a world of advanced communications and are going through some very changing economic times; therefore, outside influences are very strong. Radio, television, newspapers, or trade and professional publications carry both negative and positive news on important topics, and high-impact commercials influence people.

It is important that a speaker try to find out the morale of the group from the meeting planner. If the group is on a "high" because of an outstanding accomplishment, you should know this. On the other hand, if the group is "low" because of a recession or any bad news, you should know that also. News events the day before or the day of the meeting can make an impact. I'll never forget the day several years ago in California when I was to conduct a morning real estate sales seminar. I picked up a morning paper at breakfast and the headlines were, *REAL ESTATE SALES SUFFER BIG DECLINE*. I was able to turn this negative situation into a positive one by stressing right at the opening that we were going to work extra hard on techniques to help make more sales in a declining market. Be alert for current influences.

People in an audience have a tendency to drift and think about the outside influences. *You've got to provide a strong incentive to capture and hold an audience's attention.* The outside influences always come to the inside of the meeting room.

13. *Is the meeting room properly lighted?* Dimmed lights are okay for banquets while eating, candlelight church and/or communion services, lounges, and restaurants. However, dimmed lights are a definite detriment to effective speaking. Make sure the room is well lit and that the lights are turned up to their brightest when you speak. Trying to get a message across or trying to develop enthusiasm, inspiration, or motivation in an audience sitting in a dim, half-dark room is impossible. The chemistry between the speaker and the audience is simply not right. It's like trying to motivate or force a hippopotamus to run at full speed! The only way to develop good, effective two-way communication (speaker to audience and audience to speaker) is to have the right type of room atmosphere. The audience wants to and must see you clearly, and you should be

able to see all of the audience clearly. If you are speaking at any dimmed-light occasion, make sure you have someone alerted to turn the lights up as you are being introduced.

It's amazing how many speakers, hotel/motel convention overseers, and meeting planners don't understand the importance of having the room properly lighted. In a dimly lit room, your message will go over with the excitement of watching a turtle trying to cross the road.

One afternoon in Louisville, Kentucky, I had a most frustrating experience. I was to speak to a national franchise convention, and at the request and insistence of the meeting planner I consented to speak with the hotel meeting room dark and just a spotlight on me. I had already learned that this didn't work after a luncheon or banquet, but since this was midafternoon I thought I would give it a try. This was a mistake and another learning experience. After sixty seconds of dead silence and not one bit of response from the audience, I requested that the lights be turned on. After a minute or so, I got the audience with me. I really learned a lesson from that experience. For success with your listeners, let there be light on you and the entire audience.

14. *Does the meeting room have cool, fresh air?* A room that is too warm and filled with dead air has a negative effect upon the audience. You want the audience awake, alert, and alive so that they can get the most out of your talk. Warm, stale air encourages drowsiness, dullness, and sleep, especially after a meal. A room filled with cigarette smoke is bad also. So to keep both you and your audience fresh and alive, make sure there is ample fresh, cool air circulating throughout the meeting room. It will help you to get your message across much easier and more effectively.

15. *Is the platform area neat and professional, with nothing distracting in sight of the audience?* I've seen it happen many times at lectures and seminars that when one speaker finishes he or she leaves the platform with the chalkboard or flip chart filled with figures and drawings that he or she used to make certain points in his or her talk. The emcee goes ahead and introduces the next speaker without seeing to it that the chalkboard or flip chart is cleared. However, the next speaker is now sharing the

platform with the last speaker's illustrations. Never permit anything distracting like that to happen. The platform area in the
front of the room must be neat, clear of all papers, charts,
graphs, drawings, illustrations, figures, facts, signs, and announcements when a speaker starts his or her talk. An audience
is attracted to those things and will not resist the temptation to
look at them periodically, thus turning their attention away
from the speaker.

The audience will respond much better to you when everything around you is neat and professional, with nothing distracting their attention.

HOW TO MAKE EVERY CONDITION RIGHT
FOR YOUR SUCCESS

Make Sure Even the Smallest Detail Is Made Right
for Success

Don't leave anything to chance. Know your group with in-
depth understanding and remind yourself how the fifteen critical keys will affect your listeners. Make a firm committment to
yourself that you will always seek enough information about
the attendees to *deliver your speech with a personalized flavor.* As
Aristotle said, "The hearers are the most important aspects of a
speech situation."

If possible, obtain current knowledge about your group.
Learn all you can about conditions in advance and prepare for
any potential problems. Today's powerful television, radio, and
newspaper influences will come inside of the meeting room
with every attendee. Make every condition right for your success by being able to speak the listener's language and to bring
in at least two or three remarks that are particularly pertinent
and directly targeted to your specific audience. You win an audience by persuasion and good human engineering principles,
by talking in terms of the listeners' interest, not by force. In addition to knowing the people in your audience, you also should
know the exact impact the meeting planner wants you to create
on those particular people. Once you *know your audience* and

what must be done you are then in a position to determine *how it's going to be done,* which will be covered in later chapters.

I have written this book as a complete guide to effective speaking so that it will help you to prepare for any speaking situation you may encounter in the future. I suggest that you use a highlighter pen and highlight everything herein that pertains to you and your specific situation. If and when your speaking situations change in the future, repeat this process. Many effective speaking principles overlap and can be used effectively for many different types of situations. There are so many different speaking situations that I cannot list every one, but I assure you that when you have completed this book, you will know how to handle each one.

HOW TO FULFILL THE AUDIENCE'S EXPECTATIONS

No One Has Ever Left Home to Attend a Flop or to Hear a Failure

Think about it. Have you ever left home to attend a meeting when you knew ahead of time that the speaker was a failure? Of course not. *Part of knowing the audience is understanding that the audience wants you to be successful.* Listeners come to a meeting to hear a success. Furthermore, they will help you to be successful if you will do your part of fulfilling their expectations by providing them with a genuine, sincere speaker who has done his or her homework. To provide an audience with what they want is so simple. They want a speaker to be his or her best. They want a speaker who does not waste their time. They want a speaker who is genuine and who shows how much he or she cares about the audience. They want a speaker who respects, trusts, admires, and likes an audience. That's creating a sincere "speaker's acceptance climate" in which the speaker *earns* the loyalty of the attendees. That's when the audience will really care about a speaker and applaud warmly and generously at the end, perhaps giving a standing ovation, for a job well done!

"GARDLINES"

1. The audience will be interested in you only after you have shown honest and sincere interest in them.
2. Speak the audience's language.
3. Bring in one or two remarks at the beginning of your speech that are pertinent and directly targeted to your specific audience.
4. Deliver your speech with a personalized flavor.
5. Never think of your listeners as being living, breathing backboards for the words of your speech.
6. You win an audience by persuasion, not by force.
7. Finding out critical audience background information a few minutes before you start speaking or trying to size up the audience after you have started speaking is too late.
8. You must *earn* the audience's loyalty. You can't beg, borrow, or steal it.
9. The fifteen things you must know to create a positive audience acceptance climate:
   a. What is the exact purpose of the meeting?
   b. What is the theme of the meeting?
   c. What are the occupations of the listeners?
   d. What have the listeners been exposed to and what was their attitude toward the subject and toward the speaker?
   e. What is the overall income range of the audience?
   f. What is the educational background of the group?
   g. What is the age of the audience?
   h. Is the group male, female, or both?
   i. How many people will be in the audience?
   j. Where will the meeting be held?
   k. What's on the meeting agenda right before you speak?
   l. What is the morale of the group?
   m. Is the meeting room properly lighted?
   n. Does the meeting room have cool, fresh air?
   o. Is the platform area neat and professional, with nothing distracting in sight to the audience?
10. You must know your audience and *what must be done* before you can determine and prepare *how it's going to be done*.
11. The outside influences on an audience always come to the inside of the meeting room.

12. The audience came to the meeting to hear a success.
13. The listeners want the speaker to be his or her best and a person who does not waste their time.

THOUGHT-PROVOKING QUOTES

Effective leadership
must comprise many
elements, three of which
are essential: integrity,
enterprise, and service;
and of these, integrity
is first among equals.
RAWLEIGH WARNER, JR.

Of all the forces that make
for a better world, none is
so indispensable, none so
powerful as hope.
CHARLES SAWYER

Genius is talent set
on fire by courage.
HENRY VAN DYKE

An idea, to be suggestive,
must come to the individual
with the force of a revelation.
WILLIAM JAMES

Faith in yourself will
make despair disappear.
FRANK TYGER

The good persuader, right or
wrong, is still a good
persuader.
ROBERT HALF

Your success is not predicated
on the failure of others. When
you help others succeed, they
help you succeed.
ROBERT HALF

Happiness lies not in the
mere possession of money;
it lies in the joy of
achievement, in the thrill
of creative effort.
FRANKLIN D. ROOSEVELT

Keep your fears to
yourself, but share your
courage with others.
ROBERT LOUIS STEVENSON

To know what we must do is
good sense; to know what we
must think is intelligence.
JOSEPH JOUBERT

Hope is not a way out.
It is a way through.
STEVEN J. DANIELS

Defeat never comes to any
man until he admits it.
JOSEPHUS DANIELS

Faith that the thing can
be done is essential to
any great achievement.
THOMAS N. CARRUTHERS

We are all salesmen every
day of our lives. We are
selling our ideas, our
plans, our enthusiasms to
those with whom we come
in contact.
CHARLES M. SCHWAB

5

KEYNOTING, OPENING, CLOSING, AND LUNCHEON/BANQUET SPEAKING

Positiveness is a good quality for
preachers and orators because whoever would obtrude
his thoughts and reasons upon a multitude will convince
others the more as he appears convinced himself.

JONATHAN SWIFT

Plan Your Audience Strategy

HOW TO TAKE THE AUDIENCE'S PULSE

What Time of the Day Will You Be Speaking, at What Type of Function and in What Kind of Atmosphere?

The mark of a confident and effective public speaker is to care about doing the best job possible. Therefore, he or she pays close attention to every detail and to knowing everything possible about the subject matter. He or she tries in advance to take the pulse of the audience by knowing the environment of the meeting, the timing of the speech, and the type of function at which the speech will be given.

I urge you to study this chapter seriously and think of it as a thorough look at your listeners, helping you to better understand your audience so that you can best be prepared. This material is a follow-up and extension of the last chapter, "Know Your Audience."

This chapter is written to provide you with a more professional, in-depth guide to the highest level of public speaking. Every speaker will find it informative and beneficial. The contents will enlighten you as to what the meeting planners and chairpersons demand and want from speakers who appear on their programs. These successful, effective speaking techniques, ideas, and principles carry over from one type of speaking situation to another.

I caution you, *using good humor effectively is an art.* If you have the ability to use humor effectively, by all means use it. If you don't, avoid it. If you decide to use two, three, or more humorous stories or jokes, practice each of them a minimum of twenty-five times before you attempt to use them in public. There are thousands of public speaking occasions where humor is not needed at all. There are some speaking occasions that demand good humor. The ability to use humorous stories and jokes effectively can be developed if you have a strong desire to do so. It will take much determination, self-discipline, and practice. You must analyze yourself and decide your speaking goals. You must know your present qualifications. Speak *only* when you are at your absolute best. Practice, preparation, and hard work will take you to any level of public speaking that you seek.

Audiences respond differently at certain times of the day and at certain functions. Even though you might be preparing a talk right now for a function or situation I haven't discussed, the principles will overlap from one type of function or situation to another. Webster defines *function* as, "a special duty or performance required in the course of work or activity; to act in a required or expected manner; a thing that depends on and varies with something else." With so many different speaking functions and occasions available, it's impossible to name and list every kind of public speaking type function there is. However, by knowing how to handle the various speaking functions and situations I will discuss, you can draw parallels for your specific speech. *Many of the principles apply to all functions.* You will know what to expect from your audience, and you can then be best prepared to handle that particular situation. I realize that this is a very professional, in-depth look at an audience, but there's something here for every person who desires to speak confidently in public. Again, I encourage you to read and study this material in its entirety, because you never know where your next speaking engagement may take you.

HOW TO HANDLE THE EIGHT SPEAKING SITUATIONS AND FUNCTIONS

Opening (Kick-off) Speech

The opening of a session is as crucial as is the opening of any speech. Meeting planners and program chairpeople want their convention, sales or management seminar, all-day conference, half-day training session, one-hour employee-customer relations seminar, annual goal-setting conference, or any type of meeting started off on a high note and with a positive bang. The opening few minutes set the tone and atmosphere for the duration of the meeting. Again, I will quote some feedback letters to share the meeting planners' thinking with you so that you can benefit from their remarks. I only wish I could have had exposure to this valuable information when I first started speaking at company meetings, service clubs, community affairs, conventions, church work, and so on.

One feedback letter stated, "We had hoped that your opening address would stimulate and motivate our people to 'Turn on the juice' and it did just that." Another feedback letter said, "It is important that meetings start off correctly, and you started our most successful convention with enthusiasm, humor, and a message." I urge you to study and learn from these various feedback letters as these are "genuine quotes." It's important to know the thinking of program chairpeople and meeting planners.

I don't know what subject is best for you (you'll have to decide that, and this will be covered in the next chapter), but I can tell you that you had better pick a subject that you can deliver with lots of genuine enthusiasm and inspiration, whether the talk is for five minutes, ten minutes, twenty minutes, or an hour. A dull start for the meeting session means it usually will be dull all the way through. In opening any type of conference, you have the responsibility to build people up, to create a positive atmosphere so that the rest of the program will be received with open minds, and set the pace for a successful meeting. The success of the meeting rides squarely on the opening speaker's shoulders.

Most experienced speakers and seminar leaders love to speak at kick-offs. I love speaking at all types of functions, but especially at openings. Why? Most, but not all, opening talks are given in the morning before the group has been exposed to several other speakers. Their minds are fresh and open. They'll give you undivided and excellent attention provided, of course, you earn it.

A word of caution: If the attendees have been "boozing it up most of the night," you may have to work extra had to get the audience in gear. For opening talks, however, this is usually not a problem. For talks at other functions, alcohol can be a serious problem.

The audience loves an inspirational, enthusiastic opening talk. Their energy level is high. Don't let them down. Not only will the audience be appreciative, but the speakers following you on the program will be most appreciative also.

Closing (Wrap-up) Speech

Just as closing a speech properly is vital for the speaker, the closing speech is vital to the meeting planner. It's as important as the opening speech. The program chairperson wants the audience to leave the meeting with that "good, loyal feeling." He or she wants the program to end on a high note. Just as the close is probably the longest remembered part of a speech, the closing speech will probably be remembered longest by the attendees. *It's what the audience takes home that counts.* Regardless of its length—five, ten, twenty, or forty-five minutes—this talk should be memorable, enjoyable, and inspirational.

As a wrap-up speaker, you have a different audience now. Some closing speeches are given in the morning or evening, but the majority are given in the afternoon. The attendees are mentally tired from listening to other speakers and/or from taking part in heavy seminars or special training events. *This is no time for a speaker to read a fifteen-, thirty-, or forty-five minute heavy, factual, dry speech!!!* That type of talk will not leave the audience wanting more. That type of talk will not send the attendees home on a high note.

Here's feedback from meeting planners concerning closing talks. One wrote, "As a closing speaker for a rather lengthy session, you left them brimming over with enthusiasm." Another said, "Your closing presentation received review comments like 'enthusiastic,' 'a real pepper upper,' and 'entertaining with something to say.' It has always been particularly important to me to have my closing speech as good as the opening." Another wrote, "We asked for a 'stem winder' and that's exactly what you gave us. For the first time in memory, everyone held their seats to the very end of the conference instead of dashing for early planes." One more feedback comment: "You got their attention, you kept it, and you sent them away on a high note."

Your closing speech must be energetic, positive, enthusiastic, fast-paced with no lulls, and take the audience right along with you. That type of talk will do exactly what the program chairperson wants done. It will send the people home feeling positive, enthusiastic, and with memories of an enjoyable and profitable meeting.

Keynote Address

Webster defines *keynote* as, "A speech, as at a convention, that sets forth the main line of policy." A keynote speech could be an opening or closing speech; it could be a breakfast, luncheon, or dinner speech; or it could be scheduled anywhere in-between, such as midmorning, midafternoon, or in the evening. The keynote speech is looked at as the "main speech" or "main event." As a keynote speaker, you would certainly want to incorporate the meeting theme, reinforce the meeting planner's main points, and relate the talk to other events that have or will take place. Use any combinations of applicable guidelines that I have outlined or will outline that are applicable.

For example, here's some feedback remarks to illustrate: "Your keynote opening luncheon speech got us off on the right foot to ensure a successful meeting." Another said, "Your keynote talk (9:00 A.M.) motivated and stimulated our people and set a good pace for the rest of the conference." One meeting planner wrote, "Your keynote address at our evening (8:00 P.M.) session brought tremendous feedback. You have a beautiful way of telling a story, following up with an example and leaving them with a vivid impression of what they need to do." These are three examples of keynote talks that were delivered at different times of the day.

Cocktail Party

The best advice I can give you to save you the heartache and frustration of trying to speak at a cocktail party with an open bar is simply this—don't do it. You're only kidding yourself if you think you can win. As a speaker, you should do nothing unless you can look good doing it, get desired results, and look professional. There's just no way you can look good at a cocktail party. You will find that attendees in a cocktail party atmosphere with an open bar and drinks in their hands will not stop talking among themselves. They will continue greeting new arrivals with kisses and handshakes, and will not stop going to the bar for more drinks. Try as you may, they will not listen to you.

Breakfast and Morning Speeches

A breakfast and/or morning audience is an alert, ready-for-action type of group. The attendees are fresh, their energy level is high, they've had some breakfast and coffee, and now they are all set to go. *You've got to be ready for them.*

Such an audience is easy to motivate and inspire. They are receptive and responsive. They want to get the day off to a good start. Give your audience what they want: some good, positive, thought-provoking ideas, some enjoyment, and some inspiration. They'll love you and you'll love them.

There's one condition that can make a breakfast and/or morning meeting very difficult, and that is if it is scheduled for the morning after a big celebration or party at which too much alcohol has been consumed and the attendees didn't get to bed until the wee hours of the morning. Under those conditions, breakfast and morning meetings are extremely disappointing. Under these circumstances you look out toward the audience and, if it's a convention, you see that about half of the chairs are filled (if you're lucky) and that the attendees are deadpan and expressionless. They want and need coffee far more than a speaker. If it's a company audience, the chairs will be filled (because the boss told them to be there) with the same type of nonresponsive people. Under those conditions, do the best you can. Even under adverse conditions, any person in front of a group must put out a 100 percent effort to bring successful results. But here's one time when a speaker shouldn't be too self-critical provided, of course, maximum effort was used.

Ninety-five to ninety-eight percent of my breakfast and morning groups have been outstanding. In addition to conventions and conferences, many service clubs, company meetings, investment clubs, civic groups, businesspeople's clubs, sales and management organizations, various church groups, and professional clubs hold breakfast and early morning meetings. These are excellent groups to address.

One meeting planner said, "Your enthusiasm and positive attitude at our opening breakfast are just what we [1,000 people attended] needed to get things off and running toward an outstanding success." Another's feedback was, "Your positive message punctuated by humorous anecdotes provided the five hundred attendees with a proper ending for our convention." This breakfast speech was used as a closing wrap-up talk. I mention the number of people in attendance because many speakers feel people won't attend breakfast and early morning sessions. This is not true.

Please note this word of caution (like everything else in this book, it comes from experience): *At any meal function, don't start your talk until everyone has finished his or her meal.* Don't be guilty of falling into that trap. To make up time, sometimes the meeting planner will start the program rolling while the attendees are still eating. *Do your best to persuade him or her not to do that.* This is an injustice to the speaker. The first thirty to sixty seconds are critical. That's when you want to win the audience immediately. It's difficult to be successful in winning the audience's attention when they are still thinking about their food and trying to eat. You are interrupting them. The attendees are going to keep eating until they are through. In the next chapter, "Know Your Speech," I stress the importance of a strong opening. It's hard to win the audience over when you have given a strong opening and the attendees didn't hear it because they tuned you out while they were eating. If the audience is eating while you are talking, you usually have another distraction to overcome. The waiters and waitresses are busy coming in and out of the room either carrying in food or picking up dishes. Not only do their physical movements distract, but the clanging of the dishes is bad. The attendees almost always focus attention on anything that moves in the room instead of the speaker. Never lose sight of the fact that your goal is to capture and hold the attention of the group.

Make it one of the cardinal rules that you never touch a drop of alcohol before you speak. I know it might be tempting and inviting. Maybe you are a little nervous about giving the speech. People will want to buy you a drink. I do not know of a single *good* speaker who would touch a drop of liquor before he or she speaks. Alcohol is a depressant, and you don't need that. You need the opposite so you can arouse your listeners.

When accepting a banquet engagement, you should be cautious as to whether or not there will be a cocktail party and, if so, if it will be controlled and held within your guidelines so that you can be successful in getting your particular type of message across effectively.

For most people, too much liquor can numb their senses and slow their thinking and reaction times. Some get mellow, some depressed, some nonresponsive, and some abusive. There's only one time you can control any part of the situation, and that is at the time you have been asked to speak and when you accept the engagement. It is then that you must negotiate with the meeting planner to ensure conditions will be right for your success. Nothing is worse than watching a good responsive group be dulled into a nonresponsive group by too much to drink. Speaking to that type of group is most disappointing and frustrating. When the listeners don't respond right to the speaker, who does the meeting planner blame? You will be blamed, as the meeting planner will not blame him- or herself and the audience. Another thing to consider is that you will probably hurt your image and/or recommendation referrals from the group.

Banquet speaking is most enjoyable and gratifying when conditions are right for your success. Arrive at the meeting room early to check out equipment and to make any necessary adjustments in the room set-up. Realize your audience is tired from being active all day and that they came to the banquet wanting to be entertained. Keep your message light and use lots of your best humor. Your listeners will love you!

There are two things to watch out for that can upset the length of your scheduled speaking time, whether it is breakfast, lunch, or dinner. The first is a hotel or restaurant that is very slow in serving a meal. Some food establishments won't hire extra help to handle larger groups and some are just plain slow. A second potential problem is a meeting planner who doesn't follow through to see to it that the meal is served on time and/or has scheduled too many events for the meal period. (See additional comments under Dinner/Banquet Speeches.) More than once a meeting planner has slipped me a note saying "cut down your talk by five or ten minutes [sometimes even more]." That's rude after a speaker has prepared a talk according to the meeting planner's request and then is not able to deliver it in its entirety. However, it's best I warn you so you can be prepared, because this does happen.

Luncheon and Afternoon Speeches

Lew Sarett said, "Action is important not only for its effect upon the audience but also for its effect upon the speaker, and this applies even when before a microphone, the speaker is unseen." With a dull, colorless speaker at the podium, luncheon and afternoon audiences are susceptible to daydreaming and "the nods" after a big lunch. However, to the first-rate speaker who knows his or her audience and has prepared a talk that has action and life in it, luncheon and afternoon audiences are great speaking opportunities and are most enjoyable.

For one thing, the attendees have had some exercise, a breath of fresh air, and a break from the routine. In addition, the speaker very seldom has to fight against the effects of alcohol. An audience cannot resist listening to a talk filled with action. The listeners would be afraid that they were going to miss something.

A rule to follow when speaking to a breakfast, lunch, or dinner group is to prepare a good message on a subject you know very well and to deliver it in an entertaining, motivating, and inspirational manner. You could, of course, deliver a more basic message in the regular morning and afternoon sessions depending on the purpose of your speech and the desired impact. However, don't forget that audiences really like the speakers who can "tell their story" in a most enjoyable, inspiring, and nonboring way.

Study the following feedback from luncheon/afternoon speeches for which the meeting planner requested a solid message delivered with humor and inspiration. One said, "Your luncheon presentation was motivating, educational, interesting, inspiring, and entertaining." Another said, "Not only did your luncheon talk spark the group with a feeling of humor and goodwill, but you also gave them many good thoughts that will be helpful to all in the tough assignment of administering to the needs of our local governments." Remember, if the speaker is right, the audience will be right. If you are active and alive, the audience will be also. Tailor your talk with the right combination of message, motivation, and entertainment and you won't have to worry that the audience is going to sleep on you.

Being the last speaker of the afternoon is challenging. You can expect to find your audience tired from being in session all day and hearing several other speakers. However, that shouldn't mean they are not a good audience. You can make them a good audience with some extra effort on your part when you begin. If you think, act, and talk alive, your audience will quickly be that way also. Keep the room temperature cool and the air fresh. If the audience goes to sleep, it's the speaker's fault, not the audience's fault. Needless to say, this isn't the time of day for a speaker to stand behind the lectern and read his or her speech word for word. This is the time for a speech to be delivered with "zing" and "gusto"!

Dinner/Banquet Speeches

Under favorable conditions and when a banquet is in the hands of a first-rate meeting planner and an efficient food service staff, banquet speaking is great! Under anything less than a first-rate meeting planner and a good food service staff, it can be demoralizing and frustrating.

First, realize that most meeting planners want a banquet speaker who is humorous, entertaining, inspirational, and one who can blend in a light, positive message. When I say humorous, I mean a speaker who can tell many humorous stories and jokes, not just one, two, or three, while bringing in the light, positive message. This requires a special and unique talent. A banquet is definitely not the time or place for a dry, educational, heavy, or factual speech. People associate a banquet with a good time. They expect to be entertained and rightly so.

Depending on where the banquet is held, you may have to work in a less than desirable meeting room set-up. I've spoken in all kinds of meeting rooms, from a farm storage building to the best equipped, most plush, up-to-date motel/hotel meeting room you would ever hope to find. Most of the newer meeting rooms have first-rate speaking equipment and facilities. However, there are many meeting rooms that do not have such equipment. You must be flexible and do your best with the equipment you have at hand. The voice projection systems you encounter may rate from good to fair to nonexistent. A lecturn or podium may or may not be available. The cooks may not be able to close off the kitchen to cut down on kitchen noise. The tables and chairs may not be compact and as close to you as you would like. Perhaps the lighting or accoustics aren't the best. The air conditioning may not be working properly and the room may be very hot. It might be that your meeting room has open doorways with no way to close the openings. The challenge is to be creative and to solve these problems the best you can. Try to arrive at the meeting room, check everything, and make any necessary adjustments well before the attendees start to arrive. Of course, if you're in a first-class meeting room, you don't have to be concerned with most of these problems, but you still should get to the meeting room early and make a "mike check" and any necessary adjustments. The meeting room set-up is of primary importance, so arrive early to correct any problems you can and to make the best with what you've got to work with.

Two other prime concerns that have an influence on your audience are these: (1) the food service staff, and (2) too much alcohol. You, as the speaker, have no control over either. It's very difficult to sit at a banquet and see your *good* audience turned into a *mediocre* to *poor* audience because the establishment didn't have the meals prepared on time, because they were disorganized and very slow in the serving process, or because the attendees were served an inferior meal or one that was served cold when it should have been hot.

Poor service and poor food create a negative atmosphere with the attendees while good service and good food create a very positive atmosphere. The establishment wants to sell as much food as it can, so many times instead of a salad and main course, the banquet meal consists of a four- or five-course extravaganza, everything from soup to nuts. Such a meal takes time to serve. That's fine if the establishment serves good food without lengthy waits between each course and does not cause the meeting to run behind schedule. Excessive waits and anything other than good service and good food can dull the meeting room atmosphere.

Most of the time you can satisfactorily work through or around such problems, thus delivering your speech successfully. These listed points are concerns, but not your biggest potential problem. *Your biggest concern at a banquet is too much alcohol.*

There are many banquets at which there is neither a cocktail hour nor alcoholic beverages including wine served before and during the meal. If that's the case, you obviously don't have a problem. However, there are many banquet speeches given after a cocktail hour. If the meeting planner controls the cocktail period from thirty to forty-five minutes, you probably will not have a problem. If it's a full hour cocktail period, you've got a potential problem. If the cocktail period runs over an hour and if the bar is left open and/or wine is continuously served with the meal, in all probability you've got a real problem. Remember, the establishment not only wants to sell all the food they can, but they want to sell all the liquor they can because there's even more profit in alcoholic beverages. You are at the mercy of the meeting planner and his or her ability to control the situation. How long should you speak to a group who has had too much to drink? Even five or ten minutes is too long, and I can assure you that they will seem like an eternity. You and your speech will be as welcome to the audience as a sheepherder would be at a cattlemen's convention.

If you are trapped in this situation, make sure to turn up the lights to their brightest and that there is plenty of cool, fresh air. Keep your speech as brief as possible. Speak slowly and distinctly. Remember, your listeners' minds are dull, so don't make your thoughts difficult to follow. Keep it simple.

Evening, Neighborhood, and Community Speeches

Evening meetings are very common in every city, large or small, because it's the only time that many working people can attend. These groups can be service clubs, church groups, the school PTA, city council, town board, various farm groups, professional organizations, volunteer health groups or various auxiliary organizations.

Suitable meeting rooms are frequently a problem, as discussed under the section on dinner meetings. In addition, it's frequently impossible to estimate the attendance. At one meeting, it may be standing room only. At the next meeting, half of the chairs may be empty. This would be a good place to set up only half the usual number of folding chairs. This makes the crowd look larger and automatically arranges the attendees in a close and compact fashion, thus helping the speaker to get a better response. You can always bring out more chairs as they are needed, which will make the meeting look even more successful. If the chairs are permanently fastened to the floor, rope off a section to be used.

Be prepared for people to arrive late. Some will have to leave early because of bus schedules and baby sitting schedules or prior committments. Always prepare and practice your talk so thoroughly that you will not get upset by these distractions. Evening audiences are good, receptive groups. Know that your audience will probably be tired because they have worked all day. The speaker who goes over best is the one who is prepared, knows the audience, is brief, clear, and specific, and finishes his or her talk right on time. The audience likes an evening speaker who keeps things moving and who thinks, acts, and talks in a lively way. If you can do that, you'll be a "hit."

HOW TO TAILOR YOUR STRATEGY

Be Armed With Background Information to Successfully Meet Every Speaking Challenge

No two people are exactly the same and no two audiences are exactly the same. The speaker who will tailor his or her talk for a specific group will always go over well and be in demand.

Tailoring your strategy is not difficult if you take time to determine the critical factors about your audience.

In Chapter 4, I stressed the importance of knowing where you are speaking, to whom you are speaking, and why you are speaking to that particular group. Professional speakers go one step further and make it habit to take an in-depth look at what is the speaking function and environment and when they will be speaking so that they can fully understand and know the audience. Arm yourself with all of these pertinent facts. The atmosphere, function, and time of the event—whether it is a keynote, opening, morning, luncheon, afternoon, closing, evening, and/or banquet speech—is important so that you can sufficiently determine *how* to plan and deliver your speech to meet the specific speaking challenge successfully.

Draw from the material presented in this chapter and adapt it to your specific speaking category and then tailor your strategy. Many public speaking principles overlap in many ways and a principle explained under one heading can be made to apply to several others as well.

Now I have covered in detail the first two legs of the successful speaking triangle, *know yourself* and *know your audience*. We are now ready for the third leg of the successful speaking triangle, *know your speech,* which starts with Chapter 6.

"GARDLINES"

1. Always determine well in advance what time of day you will be speaking, at what type of function and in what kind of atmosphere.
2. The various type situations and functions:
   a. Opening (kick off) speech.
   b. Closing (wrap-up) speech.
   c. Keynote address.
   d. Cocktail party.
   e. Breakfast and morning speeches.
   f. Luncheon and afternoon speeches.
   g. Dinner/banquet speeches.
   h. Evening, neighborhood, and community speeches.

3. Don't use humor unless you are positive you have the ability to use it successfully. Using humor effectively is an unique talent.
4. Speak at only the occasions where you are your absolute best.
5. It's what the audience takes home that counts.
6. At a meal function, never start speaking until everyone has finished eating.
7. As a speaker, never touch a drop of alcohol anytime or anywhere before you speak at any function.
8. Always arrive at the meeting room early to check out speaking conditions and equipment. Make conditions as right as possible to ensure the success of your speech.
9. Always be sufficiently armed to successfully meet every speaking challenge.
10. Audiences respond differently at certain times of the day and at certain functions.
11. Tailor your strategy to each audience.

THOUGHT-PROVOKING QUOTES

Nothing is more powerful than an individual acting out of his conscience, thus helping to bring the collective conscience to life.
NORMAN COUSINS

Every man is worth just so much as the things are worth about which he busies himself.
MARCUS AURELIUS

The successful man's destiny is determined, in large measure, by what he is able to get other people to do.
LEE S. BICKMORE

When schemes are laid in advance, it is surprising how often the circumstances fit in with them.
WILLIAM OSLER

To gain one's way is no escape from the responsibility for an inferior solution.
WINSTON CHURCHILL

To be persuasive we must be believable; to be believable we must be credible; to be credible we must be truthful.
EDWARD R. MURROW

Power in the hands of the arrogant who lack character, knowledge and experience, is a sure way to failure.
HARRY F. BANKS

Whatever good there is in the world I inherit from the

courage and work of those
who went befoe me. I, in turn,
have a responsibility to make
things better for those who
will inherit the earth from me.
ARTHUR DOBRIN

Men often mistake
themselves, but they
never forget themselves.
GEORGE SAVILE

If you give yourself to
your task at once, you
won't have to do it twice.
DAVID SEABURY

Faith is building on what you
know is here so you can reach
what you know is there.
CULLEN HIGHTOWER

The biggest cause of trouble
in the world today is that
the stupid people are so sure
about things and the intelligent
folks are so full of doubts.
BERTRAND RUSSELL

We often seem more anxious
to defend our performance
than to improve it.
CULLEN HIGHTOWER

The test of leadership is not
to put greatness into humanity,
but to elicit it, for the
greatness is already there.
JAMES BUCHANAN

6

KNOW YOUR SPEECH

*Public speaking requires unquestioned
knowledge of your subject. You can not explain
to others what you do not understand.*

H. V. PROCHNOW

Select a Definite Purpose

HOW TO ELIMINATE YOUR CHANCES OF FAILING

Thoroughly Prepare and Practice

When armed with the triangle of successful speaking, anyone can learn to speak in public confidently and effectively and can have unlimited growth perfecting his or her speaking skills. The first leg of the triangle of successful speaking was *know yourself*. The second leg of the triangle was *know your audience*. To complete the triangle, this and the following two chapters will cover *know your speech*. This is an important, indispensable step in making any speech—whether it is a one-minute presentation in the board room, a speech of introduction, a report on the progress of a special fund-raising committee, or a twenty- to thirty-minute speech at a national convention. *You must know exactly what you are going to say and how you are going to say it.* I'm certain that any professional speaker will tell you that the most effective way to control stage fright and all of its many symptoms is *total preparation*. If you are totally prepared, you not only know what you are going to say but you have practiced and found the right way for you to say it, thus eliminating your chances of failing. Your progress and growth at speaking in public will be in direct proportion to your total preparation.

HOW TO ESTABLISH A SPECIFIC PURPOSE

Before You Choose a Topic, Determine a Definite Purpose

Lew Sarrett said, "If a speaker is not governed by a definite purpose, his efforts are largely wasted." In choosing the right topic for you and the audience, you must ask yourself three important questions. First, what must my speech do to have the right desired effect upon the audience as requested by the meeting planner? What is my speech goal? Which one or which combination of the five basic speech purposes listed below will fulfill the impact requirements? Second, am I right now, or can I be, fully qualified to speak on the chosen topic so that I fulfill the speech purpose? Third, what is the most effective way to organize and deliver my speech? Questions 1 and 2 will be answered in this chapter. Question 3 will be handled in this and the next two chapters.

THE FIVE BASIC TYPES AND PURPOSES OF SPEECHES

Memorize These Categories Immediately

To fulfill the goal, the overall desired effect, of the speech, I have broken down the various types of speeches into five categories. When deciding what to talk about, your first decision is to choose one of the five speech purposes or goals. If it's a combination of two categories, and it certainly could be, one should be chosen as the primary purpose and the other as the secondary purpose. I suggest that you study and memorize these five categories. Ideas about where to get speech material to fulfill these speech purposes will follow in this and later chapters.

1. A Speech to Persuade

In this type of speech, you want to convince and influence your audience to your way of thinking. You want them to see things from your point of view and still have them respect, trust, like, believe, and admire you. To win and keep the audience's loyalty, you will have to use your best human engineering and communicative principles and skills. Your goal is to open the listeners' minds, plant your ideas in their minds, and then skillfully word your speech in such a way as to keep opposing ideas from arising. He or she who can accomplish that is truly a dynamic, powerful person as well as speaker.

Here are some examples of a speech to persuade:

- You want to persuade the audience that drinking while driving is indeed a very serious condition in your area.
- You want to convince the stockholders that the company will be more profitable next year.

- You want to persuade the audience that there is sufficient interest in the community to support a community center.
- You want to persuade the entire youth convention the church should be an important part of their lives.
- You want to successfully influence the PTA audience so that they understand why certain changes have been made.
- You want to convince the judge and jury that ice on the street caused your car accident, not reckless driving.
- You want to persuade the chamber of commerce that not enough promotional material has been sent out to attract new business.
- You want to persuade the administrative church board that electric heat should be used inside of gas.
- You want to convince area farmers that the water basin program was established to help control flooding situations for the whole area, not for just a few at certain locations.

A person who is a good persuader is a very sought-after speaker as well as a leader on his or her job. This person is a professional at using a key word for leadership—*empathy*. Webster defines *empathy* as, "The projection of one's own personality into the personality of another in order to understand him better; the ability to share in another's emotions and feelings."

2. A Speech to Motivate

In this type of speech, you want to motivate your listeners into some type of positive action. You want to create the positive "want to do it" attitude in your audience about doing the thing you suggested be done rather than the feeling they "have to do it." Webster defines *motivate* as, "Some inner drive, impulse, intention that causes a person to do something or to act in a certain way; incentive, goal; to supply a motive for; causing or tending to cause motion." In this type of speech, you would want to appeal to one or more of the five major motives inside of every person—pride, profit, love, fear, and self-preservation. These are the motives that cause people to get into action. He or she who can favorably motivate an audience has the whole world with them because they know how to *reach people.*

This type of talk requires your best selling skills. Selling ideas, concepts, new procedures, or products to your audience is not difficult if you constantly practice the basic rule of talk in terms of your listeners' interests. Tell the audience how they will benefit from doing the thing that you suggest. Every person on the face of this earth is a *salesperson.* Webster defines *sell* as, "To establish faith, confidence, or belief in (to sell oneself to the public); to persuade someone of the value of something." Effective leaders are good motivators and thus good salespeople.

Children sell ideas to their parents, parents sell to their children, doctors sell to their patients, lawyers sell to their clients, ministers sell to their congregations, managers sell to their workers, businesspeople and salespeople sell their goods and services, leaders sell ideas to their followers, and so on.

Here are some examples at work, city hall, civic clubs, churchs, and conventions where a speech to motivate could be used:

- You want the listeners to change to your public relations techniques immediately.
- You want to motivate the board of directors to act without delay putting into practice your cost-efficient plan because present procedures are outdated.
- You want to motivate the group to cease opposing the project because it will only raise their taxes in the end.
- You want to motivate the group so that each member will contribute $5.00 for the new building fund.
- You want to motivate each member present to bring four prospective members to the next meeting.
- You want to motivate everyone to attend the special prayer breakfast next Wednesday morning.
- You want to motivate all the chamber of commerce members to bring their employees to the retail sales seminar next month and convince the employers that the cost is justified.
- You want to motivate all the present church members to buy a new organ from you.

- You want to motivate the listeners to vote for a certain new law.
- You want to motivate the members of the XYZ Trade Association that each should contribute $100.00 a year for a national advertising campaign.
- You want to motivate the chamber of commerce members to vote for investing $XXX for new Christmas lights.

Your success in making a motivational speech with action to follow will be in direct proportion to how well you sell yourself, how well you appeal to the audience's strong motives, and how well you talk in terms of your listeners' interests by stressing the benefits the audience will receive from doing the thing you suggest.

3. A Speech to Inform

In this fast-changing world many speeches are designed to be informative. Some speakers refer to this type talk as "a speech to educate." Most people think of informative talks as dry, heavy, dull, and boring. They don't have to be! The speaker's challenge is to make an informative talk exciting, enjoyable, and interesting.

Recently, I heard a speaker give a most informative talk on what his company saw happening in the telecommunications industry in the next ten years. This subject could have been one of those talks in which you say to yourself, "I'll be glad when that speaker is through . . . his slides, facts, and figures are boring." It was a delight to watch this speaker work. His enthusiasm, fast-paced style of delivery, earnestness, and genuine excitement made this one of the most informative, educational, memorable, and enjoyable talks I have ever listened to. When he said he was excited about the future, he got the audience excited about the future also! He made thirty minutes seem like five. That's the mark of a professional.

A facts-and-figures speech does not have to be "the same old corporate malarkey." Recently, the company president preceded me on the program, giving the company's "progress of the past year report" and the "company's goals for the next

year." This man delivered his "where we've been and where
we're going" speech with so much pride, color, and animation
that he made everyone in the audience feel proud and glad to
be part of the company. What a pleasure it is to follow a person
like that on the program. That update speech was not the dry,
dull, lifeless talk I hear so many times.

Here are some examples of informative talks:

- To educate your audience about the purpose of your favorite
  auxiliary, service club, professional group and/or charity organization.
- To explain a new personal health care idea and how it could benefit everyone.
- To let the PTA members know about a certain condition that exists.
- To enlighten the members on the latest results of research and
  development programs.
- To inform your employees of new operating policies and procedures.
- To explain to the chamber of commerce members a totally new
  retail marketing program.
- To inform the listeners of the basic requirements for admittance
  into a Shrine Crippled Children's Hospital.
- To inform the group of the changes in the new drunk driving
  law.

With proper preparation, practice, and good platform delivery, you can make your talks to inform come alive and be
memorable events in your listeners' minds.

4. A Speech to Entertain

Audiences love to be entertained. The listeners want a
speaker who can keep their *interest* and one who is *pleasant* to
listen to. Read very carefully how Webster defines *entertainment*.
He says, "to keep the interest of and give pleasure to; something interesting, pleasurable, amusing." There is a great
amount of misunderstanding between the words *entertainment*

and *humor.* Keeping that definition of entertainment in mind, you can see you do not have to be a humorist or a comedian to give an entertaining talk. You must be able to keep the listeners interested and be pleasurable to listen to. The speaker who can keep an audience entertained and who, at the same time, can get a worthwhile message across is in great demand.

A simple technique to help make an entertaining talk or any talk even more interesting and pleasurable is: Periodically bring into your talk incidents or examples out of your personal or professional life that are interesting and/or amusing. These incidents and examples must be relevant to a point you are making in your speech. Everyone can look back into his or her personal or professional life and come up with a minimum of twenty events that would provide an audience with some good, clean entertainment.

Stop and think about the entertainment you see on television. You see chefs entertaining you with their best recipes, travel shows entertaining you with their favorite vacation spots, gardening experts giving you helpful hints on the best way to raise vegetables, people being interviewed about their favorite hobby, coaches and athletes relating incidents and examples about what won or lost the game, and the fisherman discussing his big catch.

Every one of us has many different, interesting, and sometimes amusing experiences and incidents that would make an entertaining talk. Audiences love to hear incidents and examples from a speaker's life, just as we enjoy these things on television. These interesting, sometimes amusing, chunks of life will enable you to make an effective entertaining talk.

A partial list of general topics for your entertaining speech includes: hobbies, sporting events, cooking specialities, outdoor, fishing and hunting stories, lessons you have learned in life, mistakes you have made, the most humorous thing your child ever said to you, the best sermon you have ever heard, the most stupid thing you ever did, lessons you have learned the hard way, the best investment you have ever made, the best advice you have ever received, how you earned your first dollar, and so on. Pick an entertaining topic in which you are the expert and one that will be of interest to your audience. Everyone is an expert in something.

Every person can make excellent speeches to entertain if sufficient desire is within, just as he or she can make speeches to inform, motivate, and persuade. If you follow the foregoing guidelines, the audience will find your talk interesting and pleasurable. You must, of course, be properly prepared for the occasion.

5. A Humorous Speech

I urge you to read carefully every word that I have written under this category. I have seen many speakers lose their effectiveness and some fail miserably because they didn't have the ability to get jokes and humorous stories across successfully.

What is humor? Webster defines *humor* as, "the quality that makes something seem funny, amusing, or ludicrous; comicality; the ability to perceive, appreciate, or express what is funny, amusing or ludicrous." Humor is a joke, a quote, a story, or an incident that produces laughter, smiles, happy expressions on faces, and pleasant feelings. *To use humor successfully requires special skill and is a priceless asset that very few people possess.* While I believe that every person who has the strong desire can learn to give the other four types of speeches just presented, I do know that not every man or woman has the ability to use jokes and humorous stories skillfully and effectively. I've seen many speakers fall flat on their faces when their jokes and humor failed to get across successfully and failed to create the desired response.

Unless you are sure that you have this ability, telling jokes is a dangerous thing for a speaker to do. Getting *genuine laughs, not sympathy laughs,* out of your listeners is getting more and more difficult to do. I won't go into the reasons why because they are not important. It's important for you to realize that your audience expects you to be putting forth your best effort all through your speech. A joke that fails right at the start of your talk makes the audience doubtful and skeptical of your ability as a speaker and also raises questions about the worthiness of the message that will follow. It is a shame to destroy your audience's confidence in you and/or to ruin a good speech because your joke failed. I've seen many speaker's faces get red from embarrassment from the complete silence that follows a failed joke!

My advice is to accept only the speaking engagements where you feel comfortable and are best qualified.

For those of you who are qualified to use humor, here are some guidelines to follow:

1. It must be good, clean humor. If in doubt, don't use it.
2. Practice every joke or humorous story at least twenty-five times before you use it. Timing is vital. To be effective, you must work hard to have perfect timing with key words, pauses, and phrases. Test it on your friends to make sure you get the right responses before trying it on the audience.
3. Every joke should relate to the points, aims, and objectives of your speech, thus helping you to emphasize important points and helping the audience to remember your speech longer.
4. If possible, use one or two jokes directed toward your specific audience, their occupation, or profession, and/or their interests. This type of humor must be in good taste and well-intentioned. Humor used like this helps to personalize your talk.
5. The shorter the joke, the better your chances of success. A longer joke isn't necessarily better; in fact, in most cases it hurts the effectiveness far more than helps it.
6. Use just enough humor, and no more, to help achieve your speaking goal. Too much of any one thing, regardless of how good it is, is too much!

For those speakers who have the unique ability to use humor effectively, good jokes and humorous stories are an excellent way to keep the audience alert, alive, and receptive. It helps a speaker to relax the group, to lighten and liven up a heavier type of talk, to refresh the audience, and to reinvigorate the listeners to hold their complete attention.

A humorous story tied into a good, positive basic message is a popular combination at certain speaking functions. The use of humor is a skill greatly valued and widely used by some of

the best professional speakers and by some of the most promi-
nent people in the world, including Ronald Reagan.

To sum up the five types of speeches, your talk can be all of
one category or it can be a combination of categories. When
using a combination of two categories, one category should be
the *primary* purpose and the other should be *secondary*. For example, you want to make an informative talk and bring in some
entertainment. The speech to inform would be the primary
purpose and bringing in some entertainment would be the secondary purpose.

WHAT'S THE LENGTH OF YOUR SPEECH?

Don't Try to Stretch the Material

Always verify the length of your talk with the meeting
planner or program chairperson. Make sure you find out *exactly*
how long you are expected to talk. This is another key factor to
consider in accepting or rejecting the engagement offer. The
amount of material you will have to gather and organize will
naturally be dependent upon the length of time you will speak.
If you are a beginner at speaking in public, by all means do not
believe anyone who tells you, "Prepare for a ten-minute talk
and then if we find we need an extra five minutes more you can
stretch your material." *It won't work.* Chances are you'll sound
shallow and as if you didn't have the adequate material. Remember, you cannot fool an audience.

As you get more experienced, you will be able to be more
flexible with your timing because you will have a surplus of
good ideas and material, which gives you much needed *reserve
power*. While starting out, prepare for and deliver the length of
talk you have been requested and that you agreed to give.
You'll be more *confident* and *effective*. If you haven't got the time
to prepare *adequately* for the length of the talk you have been
requested to give, ask the meeting planner to find another
speaker.

Lincoln said, "I believe that I shall never be old enough to
speak without embarrassment when I have nothing to say." He

was so right. How can a speaker expect to gain confidence and become more influential if he or she goes before an audience with a mind and heart that is half prepared for the occasion? A speaker who is only half prepared deserves to feel nervous, embarrassed, and ill-at-ease.

A WELL-THOUGHT-OUT AND PREPARED SPEECH IS NINETY PERCENT SUCCESSFULLY DELIVERED

Mastery in Speech Can Only Be Reached by Mastery of One's Subject

Lloyd George said, "To trust to the inspiration of the moment—that is the fatal phrase upon which many promising careers have been wrecked. The surest road to inspiration is preparation. I have seen many men of courage and capacity fail for lack of industry. Mastery in speech can only be reached by mastery in one's subject." Mastery of one's speech will require concentration, much thought, brooding, and work. I firmly believe that a well-thought-out and prepared speech is already ninety percent successfully delivered. Preparation starts right here by knowing your specific speech purpose, your subject to fulfill that speech purpose, and the length of the talk. You are now ready to start gathering material and writing down ideas that will fulfill your speech requirements.

THE SECRET OF CHOOSING THE RIGHT TOPIC

The Right Speech Topic for You Must Come from Your Brain and Your Heart

Successful speeches are a balance of logic and emotion. I have listened to hundreds of speakers, and the ones who are successful follow this formula: Brain Power + Heart Power = Successful Speech. Those speakers have used their brain to supply the knowledge, wisdom, and logic in their speeches and they have used their heart to supply the emotion, the enthusiasm, the conviction, the spirit, the earnestness and the deep burning desire to communicate their knowledge to their listeners. Knowledge by itself is simply not enough to ensure success. Emotion by itself is not enough either. *Knowledge and emotion must be present and in balance in every speaking situation to ensure success.*

Seriously evaluate the best speakers you have heard. Aren't they the ones that had a real message and a heartfelt desire to communicate it? These better speakers made you feel as they felt: positive, happy, concerned, sad, or excited because they not only communicated with words, but they also communicated with their emotions.

WHERE TO FIND THE RIGHT MATERIAL

1. Use Your Own Experiences, Knowledge, and Expertise to the Fullest

The first place to look for speech subjects and material is inside yourself. Many beginning speakers feel that they must obtain speaking material from outside sources such as the library, civic and various government agencies, etc. They don't think about looking inside of themselves. They fail to realize the importance of looking inside of themselves first and using their own experiences and expertise and then, if necessary, going to the outside sources to obtain other people's experiences. Everything should start on the *inside* of the speaker.

For example, I delivered a forty-five minute keynote address to an audience in Minneapolis. The listeners were most warm and responsive. After the speech was over, one of the listeners approached me and asked me a question. I'll never forget the expression on his face as I completed my reply. He said, "How long did it take you to prepare that talk?" My reply, which startled him, was, "About twenty-five years." He couldn't believe it. That talk was a culmination of twenty-five years of various experiences I have had in my professional life.

I am not implying that you must spend twenty-five years preparing a talk. You have had many, many experiences and events happen in your life yesterday, last week, last month, and/or the last few years that you could use. You liked some of those experiences and some you didn't like. Some made you happy and some made you angry. Some were profitable and some were costly learning experiences. Those experiences and events in your life are where you start looking for your topics and material.

Choose a subject that you know and one that you are sure that you know. To feel confident and to be influential, choosing the right subject for you is vital. *You must be an authority on the subject.* There is no question that the greatest number of speaking engagements go to the people who have acquired the most success, skill, and expertise in their specific professions or hobbies. *You possess levels of expertise that qualify you to talk with authority about experiences and events from your personal and professional life.*

When making a talk, remember that the audience is interested in *you* (provided you earn their interest with good speaking techniques as pointed out throughout this book). They are interested in illustrations and examples from your personal and professional life, what you have learned from trial-and-error experiences, how you get certain things accomplished, why *you* feel it best to do things a certain way, why you support a certain new concept or issue, your views, your ideas, your understanding of a certain subject or policy and/or why certain events have happened to you in the past. Those things are bound to be deeply engraved on your mind. To be a confident and effective public speaker, *you must pour you, your unquestionable knowledge, and your expertise into the talk.* That's why the first place to start looking for speech material is inside of *you.*

2. Study and Research Other People's Experiences and Knowledge Until You Have Developed Expertise

You could do thorough study and research of the other people's experiences on the subject and through education become highly knowledgeable. In this case, you would include facts, data, figures, and events *you* have discovered from reliable authorities and experts on that subject. Benjamin Franklin said, "The nearest thing to a real experience of our own is to have other people's experiences brought before us in an inter-esting manner."

Use your own experiences and examples as much as you can and then, if necessary, use other people's experiences. It's only natural that the listeners want speakers who possess high levels of expertise on their subject. Many times you can use other people's experiences to back up and prove a point from your own experiences. Samuel Johnson said, "Knowledge is of two kinds: we know a subject ourselves, or we know where we can find information upon it."

3. Pick Subjects That You Thoroughly Know and That You Really Want to Share with Your Listeners

I have seen speakers who knew their subjects well but who still failed and failed miserably. Why? They were not eager to get their message over to the listeners. Their attitude about their subjects was lackadaisical. They appeared to lack a burn-ing desire to communicate their subject to their audiences. Their talks seemed like just something they had to do. The au-dience could tell that they didn't care if they gave the talk or not because they didn't totally put themselves in their talks. That is a fatal mistake.

4. Choose Knowledgeable Subjects About Which You Feel Deeply

That's the winning combination for successful, effective speaking. Choose knowledgeable subjects that come straight from the heart so that you can speak with spirit, earnestness, and deep conviction. That's the type of public speaking that will let a speaker sit down at the conclusion of his or her talk and feel good about it. That's the speaker who gets across to the au-dience and makes the audience feel the same way he or she did about the basic knowledge, message part of his or her talk.

Unless you have your heart and emotion in your talk, even though you have the best knowledge and logic, it will be dull, colorless, and shallow. That's the type of talk that puts the audience to sleep and makes an audience look at their watches hoping the end is near.

Here's an example of what I'm stressing. I worked for the Union Pacific Railroad for thirteen years. I am very knowledgeable in the areas of railroading. Yet, if someone would call me and ask me to speak on "railroading," I would have to decline the invitation. Why? Even though I am knowledgeable on the subject, I'm only half qualified to speak on the subject. I do not have any *earnestness, eagerness,* or *heartfelt desire* to speak on the subject. Therefore, I would not do it, as I wouldn't feel confident and I wouldn't be influential. The audience would spot the lack of desire and the lack of the proper spirit, and I would not be successful.

Now I'll cite the opposite example. If someone called and asked me to speak on "confident and effective public speaking," I'd immediately say yes to the invitation because it's a subject that I am knowledgeable on and I would speak from my heart with spirit, excitement, and eagerness. I would have a burning desire and earnestness to get my knowledge (logic) across. Andrew Kennedy Boyd said, "There are important cases in which the difference between half a heart and a whole heart makes just the difference between defeat and a splendid victory. I am convinced that no man or woman is ever great or does really great things without genuine earnestness."

Far too many people today do not fully understand the importance of selecting the right topic and where to get the speech material once the general subject has been decided. Many think to prepare all they have to do is take a fast glance at a newspaper, magazine article, or perhaps a book and they are ready to give a speech. Usually a speaker who prepares that way *recites* a few canned thoughts and phrases and sounds more like the *article talking* or the *book talking* than a real, live speaker talking. Some speakers that I've heard even try to present such obtained thoughts and phrases as their own, and they usually really "bomb." Why? The speech is lacking the most important element there is—*you!!* There's nothing wrong with studying and researching books, newspapers, and magazine articles, but their points, facts, and ideas must be skillfully prepared according to the requirements set forth in this chapter. A "fast glance" at something doesn't give you expertise and unquestionable knowledge of a subject. That's half-hearted preparation at best.

Quintilian said, "He who speaks as if he were reciting forfeits the whole charm of what he has written." The audience wants *your* convictions, interpretations, experiences, and spirit. H. V. Prochnow said, "Public speaking requires sincere convictions earnestly expressed. You cannot convince others of what you do not believe and feel."

GET EVERY IDEA AND FACT DOWN ON PAPER

Accumulate as Many Ideas and Facts as You Can

William J. Reilly said, "Straight thinking starts with facts. Careless thinking starts with opinions." You established the primary purpose of your speech and you have chosen the subject. You now are knowledgeable, or will be by speech time, on your subject either through your personal or professional experience or by study and research. You have heartpower, the real desire to get the subject across, and you know how long the speech is to be. Now it's time to accumulate all of the speech material you possibly can.

On a clean pad of paper, used only for your speech, write down immediately every fact, idea, analogy, definition, demonstration, exhibit, testimonial, quotation, statistic, point, illustration, event, and/or example that comes into your mind. At this stage, they don't have to be in any kind of order. Arranging your material in the right sequence will be covered in a later chapter. Right now you are concerned about getting every fact and idea about your topic down on paper. Depending on your lead time, this may take several hours of periodic thinking or it may take several days of off-and-on again thinking. Look inside of yourself for ideas first and then to outside sources for material.

Leave your speech note pad in one handy location, at the office or at home. Always carry 3 × 5 cards in your pocket or pocketbook every place you go. Use these cards to jot down ideas for your speech as they pop into your mind. You will be surprised by the many different times of day or night ideas will come into your mind. Write down the ideas when you think of them. Don't rely on your memory. You may forget. Get the ideas on note cards and then at your first opportunity transfer the notes to your permanent note pad. You'll find ideas coming to mind at coffee breaks, meal periods, driving to and from work, and many times in the middle of the night. Sometimes taking a walk is productive, bringing new thoughts, phrases, and ideas into focus, or maybe taking the phone off the hook and sitting at your desk or table in dead silence will be helpful to you. Some people I have talked to have told me that their best thinking time is while taking a relaxing shower. As you do additional study and research on your subject, make notes of worthy points. The main thing during this stage of your preparation is to leave nothing to memory, to write down everything that is related to the subject, and to keep thinking and adding words, thoughts, ideas, phrases, and sentences. Don't delete a thing. Don't hesitate to write down something you might feel is too insignificant. Sometimes those seemingly small, insignificant phrases or ideas will trigger better and more meaningful ideas later that same day or sometimes days after.

HOW TO DEVELOP RESERVE POWER

Reserve Power Builds Additional Confidence and Helps You to Be More Influential

Depending on your lead time, always make it a point to have much more material on hand than you can possibly use in your speech regardless of its length. *This gives you dynamic and powerful reserve power.* Reserve power comes from knowing far more about your topic than you can possibly use in your allotted time. Reserve power enables you to act and talk more confidently and helps you to be influential and persuasive. If for any reason you find that you cannot come up with good material, not filler, you should immediately call the meeting planner and ask for a shorter time slot and/or ask that he or she get a different speaker. As you gain additional experience, you'll find it much easier in determining the material needed for a certain length of talk.

Prepare So Well That There Is Little Chance to Fail

Lockwood-Thorpe—*Public Speaking Today* made this outstanding statement about preparation: "The best way for you to gain confidence is to prepare so well on something that you really want to say that there can be little chance to fail." There is little chance for you to fail in speaking if you follow the steps I have outlined thus far. At this point, you know your speech purpose, you have unquestioned knowledge about your subject either through your personal or professional experience or through study and research (or both), you have heartpower in wanting to get your topic over to the audience, and you know how long you are to speak. You also have a note pad containing far more points, facts, ideas, examples, illustrations, events, phrases, experiences, and sentences than you can possibly use making your speech, which gives you important reserve power. Believe me, you really know your speech thus far. Everything you've done points to *total preparation* and to a speaking success.

The balance of preparation and things to do so that you completely know your speech and are totally prepared—such as arranging your material (notes) for the greatest impact and practice and platform techniques to help you get your speech across effectively—will be covered in the immediately following chapters.

"GARDLINES"

1. You do not need to be a professional speaker or a great orator to make a successful speech, but you do have to prepare and practice thoroughly.
2. You can have unlimited growth perfecting you speaking skills.
3. If you are *totally prepared,* you know exactly what you are going to say and how you are going to say it.
4. Establish a definite purpose:
   a. A speech to persuade.
   b. A speech to motivate.
   c. A speech to inform.
   d. A speech to entertain.
   e. A humorous speech.

5. Don't try stretching the material. Know how long your speech should be and prepare accordingly.

6. A well-thought-out and prepared speech is ninety percent delivered.

7. Successful speeches are a balance of logic and emotion.

8. There are two places to find speech subjects and knowledge.
   a. Use your own experiences, knowledge, and expertise.
   b. Study and research other people's experience and knowledge.

9. Speech knowledge by itself does not guarantee success. True heartpower (emotion) and eagerness must be present also.

10. Get every fact and idea down on paper.

11. Accumulate as many ideas, facts, examples, illustrations, events, phrases, analogies, definitions, demonstrations, exhibits, testimonials, quotations, statistics, experiences, and sentences about your subject as you possibly can. Have more material on hand than you can use.

12. Reserve power builds additional confidence and helps you to be even more influential and persuasive.

THOUGHT-PROVOKING QUOTES

In the long run, we shape our lives and we shape ourselves. The process never ends until we die. And the choices we make are ultimately our own responsibility.
ELEANOR ROOSEVELT

No one is any better than you, but you are no better than anyone else until you do something to prove it.
DONALD LAIRD

Creativity is the quality of a person, not of the job he holds.
NORMAL G. SHIDLE

A great deal of talent is lost in the world for want of a little courage.
SIDNEY SMITH

"Let me light my lamp," says the star, "and never debate if it will help to remove the darkness."
RABINDRANATH TAGORE

Men who are unhappy, like men who sleep badly, are always proud of the fact.
BERTRAND RUSSELL

For of all sad words of tongue or pen, the saddest

are these: It might have been.
JOHN GREENLEAF WHITTIER

Those who have not sown
anything during their
responsible life will
have nothing to reap
in the future.
GEORGE GURDJIEFF

The perfecting of one's
self is the fundamental
base of all progress and
all moral development.
CONFUCIUS

All that we sent into
the lives of others
comes back into our own.
EDWIN MARKHAM

The successful people are
the ones who can think up
stuff for the rest of the
world to keep busy at.
DON MARQUIS

Life can only be understood
backward, but it must be
lived forward.
NIELS BOHR

Live constructively and
live optimistically.
ALFRED A. MONTAPERT

Leadership appears to be the
art of getting others to
want to do something you are
convinced should be done.
VANCE PACKARD

7

ARRANGING YOUR MATERIAL FOR GREATEST IMPACT

*Speaking without an outline
is like building a house
without a plan.*

FATHER JOHN GERONIMOS

You've Got to Be on Course Before You Can Help to
Navigate Someone Else's

HOW TO GET YOUR ACT TOGETHER

Speeches Must Be Structured to an Exact Plan

No individual would start building a house or any kind of building without a blueprint or plan showing the exact order of things that must be done for successful completion. A building starts with a solid foundation as the first step and then is erected step by step. It is not completed until that final step of putting the very last stone, rock, or brick into place. Then it stands as a whole, well-constructed, beautiful building.

The contractor "got his act together" and made his construction goal become a reality starting with just a piece of paper, his blueprint, in hand. Successful speeches are constructed the same way.

Have you ever seen an unattended boat on a lake or near a beach that had broken away from the dock and was drifting in the wind or with the tide? Unfortunately, many men and women attempt to give a speech without any definite construction plan in mind and they drift, just like that unattended boat, in all directions throughout their talk. I like to think of effective speech construction as similar to that beautiful building or perhaps just like taking a trip on an airplane. It has a definite starting point, flies in a straight line, and lands just as soon as it reaches its destination.

Speaking Success Is Not Accidental

I have observed many successful speakers and their success was not accidental. They had thoroughly thought out, planned, and constructed what they were going to say and how they were going to say it, and everything said was properly placed in their speeches for the greatest impact. Many have told me that as they were arranging their material they imagined that they were in front of an audience and in their minds they tested how the various points would sound. They practiced their speeches silently, mentally, and out loud to find the exact right way to communicate their various speech points and to make sure they were in the correct order. They not only rehearsed the interesting parts of their speech, but they practiced giving the noninteresting parts as well, turning *cold facts* and *statistics* into colorful, captivating, and enjoyable points so that they would be long remembered.

In sum, their success was not accidental. There was no darting or drifting from one point to another. They had a starting point and a concluding point, and the material moved in a straight line from one point to the other.

Arthur Edward Phillips in *Effective Speaking* said this about how to convey "something to say":

> The common error in regard to speaking is the assumption that all that is necessary is to have "something to say." Utterly false! Unless that "something to say" is said in accordance with the laws of the human mind which govern conviction, it might as well be spoken to the winds. The modern speaker must realize that besides "something to say" he must learn how to best convey it. He must remember that the Chathams and the Websters and the Beechers not only had "something to say" but they realized that careful study had to be given to the order and manner of its presentation.

Any time anyone stands in front of an audience with "something to say," it must be conveyed properly.

Analyze All Your Facts and Ideas

In the last chapter, I suggested that you decide your overall speech purpose and then think about and write down, not in any order, every fact (be sure they are facts, not assumptions or unproved opinions and/or claims) and idea that came to your mind to help fulfill your overall speech purpose. Now you must accurately organize your material to get your message successfully across to the audience and create the maximum impact.

The way to construct your speech successfully can be summed up in one sentence: *All relevant material must be reduced to the simplest form, placed in a logical, correct sequence, and made brief, clear, and specific.*

Dr. Edward Everett Hale suggests,

Before a speaker faces his audience he should write a letter to a friend and say, "I am to make an address on a subject, and I want to make these points." He should then enumerate the things he is going to speak about in their correct order. If he finds that he has nothing to say in his letter, he had better write to the committee that invited him and say that the probable death of his grandmother will possibly prevent his being present on the occasion.

That is excellent advice.

THE ANATOMY OF A SPEECH

The Three Basic Parts of a Speech

Regardless of the length of the talk, be it five, ten, fifteen, or thirty minutes in length, there are three main parts to every speech. They are:

No. 1. The Opener
No. 2. The Body
No. 3. The Close

This three-step formula will serve as an outline for any speech purpose. Briefly, you open the listeners' minds and tell the audience what you are going to tell them, then tell them, and then tell them what you have told them. Naturally, you will want to vary the opener, the body, and the close according to your *exact speech purpose* and the *particular type of group* you are addressing.

Be Brief and Genuine with Your Thank You, Acknowledging the Dignitaries, and Honored Statements

The first thing you would do, of course, is to make a brief and sincere thank you statement showing appreciation to the introducer and/or to the person or people who invited you to speak. If you feel honored by being asked to speak to the group, make a brief and sincere honored statement to that effect. Be brief and sincere when you acknowledge the dignitaries.

Many people in the audience will not tune in and wholeheartedly listen to a speaker when he or she is in the *thank you, mention the dignitaries* and *honored* part of the opening. They are aware that this is simply a routine. It can be overdone. Make it brief and get right into your opener so that you earn the audience's undivided attention as quickly as possible.

Memorize the following:

    No. 1. The Opener
        a. Open the listeners' minds—secure undivided attention
        b. Keep their minds open—a brief preview
    No. 2. The Body
        a. Present logically arranged major points
        b. Have each point reinforced with backup material
    No. 3. The Close
        a. Make a brief review of topic and major points
        b. Conclude conclusively

Your Speech Material Must Fit Your Time Slot

Regardless of how many minutes your speech is, if it leaves your listeners wanting more, you have been successful. Your goal now is to arrange your material so well that when you stop talking the audience hasn't had enough of you and your speech. A five-minute talk can be made to seem like a long thirty minutes. On the other hand, a thirty-minute speech can be made to seem like five minutes. *The key is the proper balance and diversification of quality, relevant material.*

In a short five-minute talk, which is about the time allowed at various civic meetings, PTA, company and/or church meetings, you would have adequate time for one or possibly two major points along with your reinforcement material. If you tried to crowd in four or five major points, your speech would seem hurried and sketchy. It would not create the right impact because you inadequately covered too much ground.

On the other hand, if you used one or two major points

with backup material in a twenty-minute talk, your talk may seem incomplete and very shallow because you left out important subject matter and perhaps didn't cover the entire subject adequately. So much depends on the type of talk, its purpose, your background, and your ability to organize and deliver a speech.

Many times I am asked, "What can I say in two or three minutes?" *Plenty,* if it is well planned and thought out. After all, many TV and radio commercials are twenty or thirty seconds and some are one minute and each spot contains the right balance of material to create the desired impact.

Sort Out Essential, Quality Material

Let me give you an analogy to stress the importance of essential material. I travel constantly and learned from experience a long time ago that I cannot check my luggage with an airline because once it is lost, there is very little chance it will catch up with me. So I have learned to live up to seven days with a small hand-carried case that fits under the seat and one small suit bag. It took practice, but I can now do it, manage with it, and have clean clothes every day. Yet, have you observed the amount of luggage carried by the average person on a seven-day trip? Staggering! That person probably would be carrying many nonessential clothes that never get worn in at least two large suitcases plus a hand-carried case. The difference is that I have learned to sort out and carry with me just the essentials.

This is exactly what speakers must do when laying out their speeches. Arrange all quality, essential material to coincide with the time frame of the speech and discard the nonessential, unqualified material.

I can't tell you how long you should speak because there are many factors to take into consideration. As you grow in public speaking, you'll naturally be able to handle the longer speeches, but remember this regardless of how good you get to be: First, a longer speech doesn't necessarily guarantee it's better. In fact, the shorter your talk is, the more chance you have at success, provided you have covered your subject adequately. Second, stop talking while the audience still wants more. Conclude conclusively at the peak of your talk, or as the old expression goes, "Always leave at the height of the party." Third, build your speech with the proper balance and diversification of material to fit your exact time slot.

A General Guideline to Follow

It is most difficult to say an *opener* should be exactly so long, the *body* so long, and the *close* so long. You will learn that from your personal speaking experiences and from your feel for the subject and the speech purpose how much material must go into each speech part. Be flexible. As a general rule and guideline to dividing your allotted speaking time, I suggest this:

    5%–10% The Opener
    80%–90% The Body
    5%–10% The Close

This is a reasonable guide to follow. Your personality is a factor. Your style, your rate of words per minute, and your subject are all factors. The main thing to remember is to *use just enough material, and no more, to accomplish your objective.*

HOW TO SELECT YOUR MAJOR POINT(S)

Plan "The Opener" and "The Close" After You Have Organized "The Body"

Keep the following formula in mind while you are sorting and evaluating your material for the body of your speech:

    The Body
    A. Present logically arranged major points
    B. Have each point reinforced with backup material

Define and Arrange Your Major Points in a Logical Sequence

After looking over and studying all of your essential, quality notes, decide on the major points. On a clean pad of paper, start writing down your key points, leaving lots of room between each major point so that when your outline is completed you can start writing down your reinforcement material underneath each major point. Concentrate and plan this outline very carefully. Decide exactly how many major points you can adequately make in your allotted time and what they are. *Get them all down on paper.*

As you are making your outline with the major points, mentally see yourself making those points to an audience. Try to imagine how the points will sound and determine if the points are clear and arranged in a *logical sequence.* If necessary, rearrange and get them in a logical sequence to make your speech easy for the audience to follow. *Everything must be in its proper order.*

FIFTEEN WAYS TO MAKE MAJOR POINTS INTERESTING, BELIEVABLE, AND VIVID

Use a Variety of Reinforcement, Back-Up Material

Now that your major points are decided, you must determine the best material to use to make your major points believable, interesting, valid, meaningful, and vivid. Try to use several of the different listed forms of material to keep your listeners' attention and to keep your talk from becoming dry and boring. Some people like exhibits and demonstrations while others don't. Some people like statistics and facts while others don't. By using a mixture of back-up material, you'll be able to hold the interest of your entire audience. You also should keep the purpose of the speech in mind when deciding on your back-up material.

1. *Facts.* Many speakers lose their credibility because they confuse facts with claims and promises. Webster defines a *fact* as "a thing that has happened or that is really true; a thing that has been or is; the state of things as they are; reality; actuality; truth." When a speaker makes a claim or promise, he or she should prove that point immediately. Webster defines a *claim* as "a statement as a fact of something that may be called into question," and *promise* as "a basis for expection."

When a speaker proves a claim or promise, it becomes a *fact* in the minds of the listeners because it is accepted without mental reservation. Claims and promises are turned into believable facts by *proof,* which Webster defines as "the art of proving; the establishment of the truth of something; to convince one of the truth, conclusive evidence" and by *evidence,* which Webster defines as "something that tends to prove; ground for belief."

Remember, the audience will not believe a claim or promise until it is proven. Then it will be accepted without any mental reservations. When you are proving claims and promises, never say, "I'll prove to you." That's bad. You are putting the audience on the defensive. You have said you are smarter than they are and that means trouble. Instead, just do it. Start with some empathy and then bring in your evidence for proof. For example, "I felt just like I know you people feel until I took a look at all of the evidence. When I saw the demonstration that I am going to conduct for you, it helped to clear up my mind. Let's take a look at it and see what conclusions we can make."

Always be prepared with evidence and proof to turn any claim or promise into a believable fact in the minds of the listeners.

2. *Exhibits.* While many talks do not require an exhibit, others could be made to be clearer, more colorful, and more captivating if an exhibit would be used effectively. Exhibits can help you to arouse suspense, build your talk to a spellbinding climax, and help you to prevent any misunderstanding. One time seeing something is worth a thousand words of description. I've seen many audiences really come alive at the time the speaker took out his or her exhibit.

In determining whether or not you want to use an exhibit, you would want to consider the length of the talk, the seating arrangement of your audience, the size of the exhibit, the size of the group, and the size of the room. If you decide to use an exhibit, here are a few guidelines to follow:

a. Before you start speaking, place your exhibit where you can reach it easily and yet in a place where it is not in sight to the audience.

b. Pick up and use your exhibit to help get your major point across. Timing is important. Make sure all the audience can see it. When the audience yells out, "We can't see it," you are annoying them rather than holding their interest. Keep it in front of the audience just long enough to create the desired impact and then place the exhibit back down out of sight from the audience.

c. When holding your exhibit, it's easy to talk to the exhibit and ignore the audience. Don't let that happen to you.

d. Practice and make every move look professional. Before an audience is no place to find out that your talk and exhibit aren't coordinated.

Exhibits not only add interest to your speech, but they offer splendid evidence and proof of a major point in your talk. The audience will remember you and your important, emphasized point much longer also.

3. *Testimony of other people's experiences.* Quote a few findings from a well-known expert source if possible. Give a brief background as to why the expert source is an authority on the subject. If you are unable to do that, get testimonial letters from the best sources possible. Read *just enough information* from these letters to help you reinforce your point. Keep it moving, and don't let there be any lulls while you are reading.

4. *Quotations.* The better known the person you are quoting, the more value the audience will put on the quotation and thus the more emphasis on your major point. Long, drawn out quotations are easily forgotten and can bore an audience, so use only those that are short and precise. Remember, their purpose is to be back-up material, not your whole speech.

For example, if I were giving a talk and one of my points is the importance of courage, I could quote Winston Churchill: "This is no time for ease and comfort. It is the time to dare and endure." These are two, short, powerful sentences that could add tremendous strength to my major point.

Let's say I'm giving a talk on freedom. I've made definition and mentioned my back-up material. I could top it off with a quote from Lyndon Baines Johnson: "Until every American, whatever his color or wherever his home, enjoys and uses his franchise, the work which Lincoln began will remain unfinished."

Quotations are everywhere. You'll find them in magazines, trade publications, libraries, and newspapers. Bookstores have many books of quotations and the subject matter of many of those is broken down into categories.

Quotations can add to your expertise, because the people you are quoting say and feel the same way about your major point as you do. If possible, try to quote well-known names. If not, you will have to give a very brief explanation about how the person you are quoting is an authority on the subject.

5. *Demonstrations.* "I am satisfied that we are less convinced by what we hear than what we see," said Herodotus. Refer to the guidelines I set forth for using an *exhibit.*

An audience likes action and things happening right before its eyes. A properly timed demonstration will do a fine job of proving your point and will help to make your talk more colorful and vivid.

Sometimes you can get a member of your audience involved in the act. That's good. Your audience will love it.

If your talk is the type that could make use of a demonstration, by all means use it. You will be more convincing.

6. *Visual Aids (Slides, Chalkboards, Films, and Flip Charts).* When used properly, visual aids do a tremendous job of helping to capture the audience and to make your points clearer and more vivid. They can be used to bring in important *illustrations, diagrams, facts,* and *figures* to help you put some *showmanship* into your talks. Visual aids not only add interest to your various points, but again, one time seeing something is worth a thousand words of description.

Make sure all equipment is present and has been placed in the right spot, has been focused, and has been *thoroughly checked out* before the session starts. There is a danger to consider every time electric equipment is used. It may fail during your presentation. Have back-up bulbs, fuses, and so on, on hand ready for quick use if needed.

I have seen many speakers flop because their equipment wouldn't turn on when they were ready for it. I've also seen some speakers attempt to use a flip chart or overhead projector only to find that their pens were out of ink. Some were going to write on the chalkboard and had no chalk and eraser present.

Use the guidelines under item 2, "exhibits," for using any of the mentioned equipment. Make sure everyone can clearly see and hear all of the presented material. Timing and coordination are most important. Talk to the audience and not to the equipment. When your point has been made, turn it off immediately (or erase it) and continue on with your speech. It's easy for a talk to drag when using these various types of equipment, but your challenge will be to keep things moving with spirit and conviction.

7. *Definitions.* In making your talk clear and holding misunderstanding to a bare minimum, consider making a brief definition of the word or term that might not be clearly understood by everyone. I recently heard one person approach another by saying, "How do you feel about the international crisis?" The other person said, "That depends on what you mean by international crisis."

When I conduct management seminars, I start each by building a foundation on a common definition of management. In asking the attendees to write down their definitions of management, it's startling how many different interpretations there are of the word *management.* Practically everyone has a different definition, enough so that my seminar would not be totally effective unless I cleared up the meaning.

The first thing I do is define a common, working basis of the term "management" so that everyone understands. Without this common definition, I would have a breakdown in communications with my attendees. There would be misunderstanding, wasted time, room for argument, and very little would be accomplished in a solid, positive way. Everyone would be interpreting what I said differently, according to his or her own definition.

Speakers must include definitions as part of their speeches on any subject or point that might be controversial or about which there could be varying ideas and opinions in the audience.

8. *Poems.* Within guidelines, poems can serve a very useful purpose in creating inspiration and/or backing up a speaker's major point in a memorable way. Poems can put some variety in your speech. Many speakers, however, get into trouble because they choose long poems that make it difficult for the audience to grasp the whole thing and/or their delivery lacks eloquence, thus cutting down on the effectiveness of the poem. Poems should be as short as possible, delivered in a genuine, captivating manner and, of course, they must be relevant to the point that is being made.

Effectively making a poem say and mean what the poet meant when he or she wrote it is an art. It takes much practice to be able to convey the real thought and feeling of the poet. Mark Van Doren wrote, "The important thing about a poem is the reader."

A poem can be an excellent way to create a change of pace in your talk. It can be a powerful and emotional opening or close for your speech as well. If you have the ability to use a poem to obtain your desired results with an audience, by all means use poetry. Otherwise, don't. If poems are merely *recited* from memory or from reading, your responses will not be good. If you can put your heart and soul into the poem and thus be very expressive, you'll get an excellent positive response.

9. *Contrasts.* Making things appear to be sharply different is an excellent way to be dramatic and convincing. Contrasts help to make your point clearer and more dramatic.

For example, one of my favorite contrasts in a motivational speech is, "You can be a *creature* of circumstances or you can be a *creator* of circumstances." Another one, "The person who really wants to do something finds a *way*, the other kind finds an *excuse*."

President John F. Kennedy said, "Ask not what your country can do for you; ask what you can do for your country."

10. *Examples.* Tell the audience stories citing actual exam-

ples involving people and things. Audiences love that. Why? Because people love to hear about the experiences of other people; *what* happened, *why* it happened, *who* was involved, *where* it happened, *when* it happened, and *how* it happened. To help you reinforce your point, the examples must be true, relevant and given with sufficient detail so that the example is complete. A good rule to follow is that it must answer the following: who, what, where, when, how, and why.

A genuine example delivered with just enough details to make it complete is an effective way to add strength and power to your talk and to help the audience grasp your ideas, enabling you to put your point across competently. When an example is cited with *specific details,* it adds believability and credibility to your talk.

11. *Analogies (Comparisons).* Webster defines *analogy* as, "similarity in some respects between things otherwise unlike; an explanation of something by comparing it point to point with some similar; similarity in function between parts dissimilar in origin and structure." In short, the speaker compares the unknown to the known or the unfamiliar to the familiar.

An analogy is an effective tool for a speaker to use when he or she is not sure that the audience will understand a term, feature, characteristic, function, the article itself, and/or a procedure. The speaker merely states the correct, unknown terminology to the audience and then follows immediately with a brief explanation relating it to something very common that everyone in the audience would understand.

For example, one position I held when I worked for the Union Pacific Railroad was as a train dispatcher moving trains over the railroad with a C.T.C. machine. Most people are not familiar with a C.T.C. machine, so I would say something like this, "C.T.C. stands for Centralized Traffic Control. A Centralized Traffic Control machine shows the actual position and movement of every train on a particular segment of track. It compares with and is similar to the function of today's common air traffic controller's radar screen, which shows the controller exactly the movement and positions of all airplanes in a certain area."

In this day and age, air traffic control is a commonly heard term and most people have seen pictures in newspapers or on television programs showing a controller keeping watch of air traffic on his or her radar screen. If they haven't seen pictures, they have read about air traffic controllers in news articles.

It's common today to see and hear advertising stressing the quickness of computer reaction time compared to the human mind, the tremendously fast air speed of a jetliner compared to the speed of sound, and the strength of martinis compared to potent drugs.

If you doubt that your terminology will be clear in your listeners' minds, an analogy or comparison is an effective tool to make your point crystal clear and to prevent any misunderstanding.

12. *Statistics.* Statistics are easily forgotten unless they are presented in a colorful, vivid, easy-to-remember way. It's much better to state a few well-presented statistics than it is to present a lot of statistics in a dry, dull way. Always try to dramatize your statistics and make them memorable and impressive so that they will stay in the minds of your audience.

For example, a leading manufacturer of cowboy boots wanted to emphasize the length of time they had been in business. Their ad started out, "When Henry Ford introduced his famous Model T in 1909, my grandfather had been making boots for thirty years!" This was an excellent way of dramatizing the number of years the company has been in business.

Many times dates can be tied into well-known events such as, "Mrs. Smith started manufacturing her secret hair coloring formula in 1941, the year the Japanese bombed Pearl Harbor and the United States began fighting World War II."

"This building is XX feet wide and XX feet long and contains XXX square feet. So that you can accurately visualize the size of the building, it would be a one-story building and would entirely cover one full city block."

Often you can use an analogy to help emphasize your statistics. "This airplane is 300 feet in length. That means it would just fit on a football field with the nose being on one goal line and the tail on the other goal line."

"This airplane will seat 296 people. I was born and raised

in a community that had a population of 295. That means that airplane will carry my whole hometown and have one extra seat left over. Since most of you are from small, rural communities, you can easily visualize the size of the airplane."

Dull, dry speeches are the ones where the speaker forgot the power of *picturesque language,* the kind of language that makes speeches come alive, be interesting, and be a lot more convincing.

Statistics are vital in substantiating claims and helping to persuade an audience. If your type of talk calls for statistics, use them wisely and express them well. Without the backing of statistics, your talk becomes nothing more than unfounded opinion.

When using statistics, by all means cite the authority. The better known the source of your statistics, the more confidence you will gain from your listeners. You should always be precise, accurate, and definite, making sure that nothing is fuzzy or cloudy. There's an old expression that goes, "If it's fuzzy in the pulpit, it's real cloudy in the pew!" Specific statistics backed up by a well-respected source will help you to be most influential with your audience.

13. *Restatements.* A technique that many professional speakers use to put importance on a certain point is to restate the important point using different phrases and different reinforcement or back-up material. When properly thought out and executed, restatement is a powerful, convincing tool to place a great amount of emphasis on a particular point.

14. *Question-and-answer periods.* This is mentioned here because if there *absolutely has to be a "question-and-answer period,"* now's the time to prepare for it while you are in the planning stage of your talk. You must gather your material to arm yourself with the answers to every possible question you might be asked.

I am very much against such sessions and suggest you decline when asked to conduct one. *These sessions are anticlimatic.* For every question-and-answer period that I could rate as *productive,* there have been twenty that would have to be rated as disasters and very nonproductive. I've seen many speakers do an outstanding job with their regular talk only to have the positive, favorable impact, lessened or wiped out because of a question-and-answer period.

I have heard some speakers say, "If I run out of material, I'll conduct a question-and-answer period for the rest of my allotted time." *Don't be guilty of that.* I have heard meeting planners say, "If we are running ahead of schedule, we can have the speaker conduct a question-and-answer period." Profitable results are difficult to obtain under the best of preparation, let alone the conditions I have just mentioned.

Two things usually happen when conducting a question-and-answer session, and they both place the speaker in a no-win situation. First, there can be a long pause with no questions being asked, thus causing the room to be filled with silence. Long quiet pauses kill a speaker fast, and the audience then senses that there was very little of interest in your talk, making you look bad even though the audience found your talk enjoyable. Instead of ending your talk with success, you now end it with failure. Second, there often are three or four people in the audience who want to show their intelligence and knowledge by monopolizing the entire session with their questions. They get their feelings of importance by trying to impress the audience and/or perhaps even by making the speaker look bad. They want to argue a certain point. They insist that you talk in terms of *their interests,* which may not be and probably isn't, in the interest of the whole group. So you'll find yourself talking to three or four people instead of to the entire group, and the first thing you know half of the audience has become bored and fed up with the whole procedure and has gotten up to leave. The *whole audience* will not be ignored for long!

I recently saw this happen in Louisville, Kentucky, where the speaker lost control because of two or three people who monopolized the period and caused people to start leaving immediately. The whole positive atmosphere of the meeting was destroyed by a fifteen-minute question-and-answer session.

The best way to handle this during your speech is to mention that if anyone has any questions about the material, you'll be in the room for a few minutes after you finish and that you would be happy to talk to them individually.

If you feel that you must conduct such a period with such possible serious consequences, and knowing that the odds are clearly against you, gather plenty of material, stay in control, limit the time you spend talking to one person, and pray that your audience stays in the room and doesn't get up to leave.

15. *Hand-Outs.* Depending on the type of speech and your exact purpose, hand-outs (illustrations, charts, samples, pictures, outlines, graphs, brochures) can be an effective way to make the audience remember you and the important points you emphasized in your talk. Hand-outs are something the listeners can take home for further information or for a review of your speech highlights. Or they could be samples that can be tasted, felt, or tried out.

Unless hand-outs are distributed at the right time, they can become very distracting. You can rest assured that the minute hand-outs are passed to the audience, the listeners are going to start reading them, looking at them, fumbling them, and in some cases they will start whispering. You stand to lose the attention of the audience. I often have seen speakers have long delays and lulls in their speeches while waiting for the hand-out material to be placed in the hands of the listeners. *Remember, when the speaker isn't speaking, the audience will be.* Unless hand-outs are distributed properly, the speaker stands to lose the attention of the audience.

Hand-outs can be an effective tool to reinforce major points. I'll explain ways to distribute them effectively in the following chapter, which covers effective speech delivery techniques.

ALL MAJOR POINTS AND REINFORCEMENT MATERIAL SHOULD NOW BE OUTLINED

Run Over the Complete Outline Aloud, Timing Yourself

After you have silently and mentally determined the major points you want to make in a logical sequence and have picked out the best back-up material, get off all by yourself and go over the talk outline several times, speaking aloud. *Be sure to time yourself so that you know you have the proper amount of material.* This serves as an excellent check to make sure the body of the speech is well-organized.

All through the sorting and construction process, keep your opening and closing material in mind. You want an opener that will stand out and immediately grab the audience. You want a close that will be conclusive and memorable. As you are reviewing your notes for the body of the speech, ideas will come to mind for your opener and close. Be sure to jot down all of them on separate pieces of paper. After serious thought, determine the best ideas for your opener and for your close. Opening and closing techniques directly follow in this chapter.

FIFTEEN CAPTIVATING OPENING TECHNIQUES

The Audience Is Usually Won or Lost in the First Few Sentences

First impressions and your opening words are vitally important. Your opening words must be well-chosen according to *Public Speaking Today* by Lockwood-Thorpe: "In public address, it is all important to make a good start. In the whole hard process of speech-making, there is nothing quite so hard as to make easy and skillful contact with an audience. Much depends upon the first impressions and opening words. Often an audience is either won or lost by the first half dozen sentences of a speech." Therefore, thoroughly know and memorize your opening statements.

The following should be considered when planning the opening of your talk. They are self-explanatory. Be brief, and regardless which one (or any combination) you use, it must pertain to and be relevant to your talk. *The total purpose of your opening statements should be to open the audience's mind, to get the audience thinking with you, and to get the audience involved in your talk.* That's securing their undivided attention!

The Opener

A. Open the listeners' minds—secure undivided attention

1. Ask a question.
2. State a startling or shocking fact.
3. Arouse curiosity.

4. Show that something is wrong.
5. Use a dynamic quotation from the Bible or a famous person.
6. Compliment the audience.
7. Use an analogy.
8. Tell a joke. (You are on thin ice unless you have a unique ability.)
9. Use a startling exhibit.
10. Refer to the occasion or the meeting theme.
11. Use a very brief illustration or example.
12. Make a short, colorful demonstration.
13. Quote the headlines of a newspaper or magazine article.
14. Use a dynamic poem.
15. Stress importance of your topic to your listeners' interests.

Never start your talk with any kind of apology. I covered this point in Chapter 2, but it is worth repeating here because it is a serious mistake that many speakers make.

Many speakers don't realize that they have the group's attention for about five to ten seconds immediately after they have been introduced. That comes automatically right between the last word of the introduction and the first word spoken by the speaker. At that point, the audience has no reason to dislike the speaker. That's why the right things have to be done immediately to capture and hold that interest. Once you have lost the interest by doing something wrong, it's difficult to win back the interest.

B. Keep their minds open—a brief preview

Immediately following your mind opener, in one or two sentences state the highlights, the main point, or the name of your talk and your purpose in addressing the group.

For example, "This evening I will share with you some ideas that will help you to turn even more minuses into pluses," or "My basic purpose this afternoon is to give you some additional selling tools to help you increase your sales."

Some speakers skip part A of the opener and start their talks directly with part B, the brief preview. That is risky. Don't forget that part A of the opener is the mind-opening phase to secure undivided attention for everything else that follows.

Here's an example: Let's say I'm speaking to a group of salespeople and my opener consists of just part B, the preview. "My basic purpose this afternoon is to give you some additional selling tools to help you increase your sales." There is a very good chance that some salespeople in the audience would say to themselves, "I'm not interested."

Now, let's start with part A and see what happens, "Company sales plunged thirty-five percent last month. This is serious. For the company to survive and for the salespeople to retain their selling positions, closing ratios must improve as prospects are becoming fewer." Now I could give part B and be assured that I have opened their minds and that I have kept their minds opened ready for the body part of my talk.

In summary, opening statements make or break a speaker. Know thoroughly how you are going to open your talk, practice it, and memorize it. It's too important to leave to chance.

SEVENTEEN SKILLFUL, STRONG WAYS TO CLOSE

Be Conclusive and Memorable

You want the listeners to remember you favorably and for a long time. The close should be the beautiful wrapping on the package, the dessert, the thing that really tops off your whole presentation.

"I guess that about wraps it up," "I guess that's about all that I have to say," "I guess I should stop since I'm about out of time," or, "I guess I'm finished." You guess??? If you don't know you're finished, you are *really* finished! Those are common phrases you hear every day. I call it the "I guess" close.

Then there is "the circle" close. The speaker who gives this type of close can be compared to an airplane that continues circling the field waiting for and trying to find a spot to land. When this speaker is all through with the body of the talk, he or she continues the circling process by going back over already presented material again and again, never spotting a place to land. A speaker who circles the field trying to close doesn't realize that he or she has already made a crash landing with no survivors on board! The speaker and the speech both crashed.

Speakers who are guilty of the I guess or circle closes usually lack confidence and audience interest. They show a pitiful lack of preparation, practice, and purpose.

The professionals agree that the close will probably be remembered the longest. It should be something that will have a positive impact on the audience. As with the opening, your closing words should be well chosen and you should know thoroughly and exactly how you are going to close your speech before you ever start. *Your close should be memorized.* It is far too important to wait until you are in front of an audience and then try to build a close while you are delivering your speech. The speaker who does that is like the person standing on quicksand in the river. He could find himself in a serious, desperate, and helpless situation.

Victor Murdock said, "If you happen to be one of a circle of speakers who are relating their experiences, you will often hear some one remark apropos of the proper construction of an address. 'Get a good beginning and a good ending; stuff it with whatever you please.'" Perhaps this statement is a little light on the purpose of the "speech body," but Murdock is right on target with the opening and close.

The following techniques should be considered when you are building the close of a talk. To help you to conclude properly, these techniques would be used immediately after your brief review of the topic and major points. You would, of course, want to use the technique that helps you to fulfill the speech purpose.

The Close

A. Make a brief review of topic and major points

B. Conclude conclusively

1. Appeal for the positive action—state in one or two sentences the action you want the audience to take followed by one sentence stating their benefits in doing the thing you suggest.

2. State your final conclusion.
3. Tie your close to an opening statement.
4. Ask a question.
5. Tell a joke—leave the audience laughing (if you have that unique ability).
6. State a startling or shocking fact.
7. Use a dynamic quotation from a famous person or the Bible.
8. Use an analogy.
9. Use a climatical poem.
10. Use a climatical exhibit.
11. Emphasize something important about the occasion or stress the theme of the meeting.
12. Pay a sincere compliment.
13. Use a short, colorful demonstration.
14. Stress the importance of your topic to your listeners' interests.
15. Use showmanship to prove your main point.
16. Summarize stating the one most important idea of your speech.
17. Quote the headlines of a newspaper or magazine article.

A Formal Announcement That You Are Going to Close Isn't Necessary—Just Do It

You don't have to tell the audience you are going to close your talk—just go ahead and do it. They will know you are closing. Don't make your close fuzzy, don't apologize, and don't stretch it out. Make it clear and concise according to your overall speech purpose.

Some speakers stop talking and sit down right after they finish with their major points and back-up material. Don't be guilty of that or your talk will sound incomplete and leave the audience dangling. Leaving off the close can be compared to going to a football game in which the most exciting part of the game was the last couple of minutes—that's when the winning touchdown was scored and you missed it because you left the game halfway through the last quarter. If you leave off the close, the audience will miss what should be the best, strongest, and most memorable part. *Conclude conclusively.*

THE MAGIC OF SIMPLICITY

Use Various Opening and Closing Techniques

You can vary and mix your opening, body, and closing material so that you fulfill the purpose of every type of speech. To review:

1. A speech to persuade.
2. A speech to motivate.
3. A speech to inform.
4. A speech to entertain.
5. A humorous speech.

There is magic in the divinity of simplicity. The secret to building any one of these talks is to make sure that all material is relevant and reduced to the simplest form. The material must be in a logical sequence and presented in brief, clear, and specific terms. Monroe said, "Have something you want to say. Want someone else to understand it. Say it as simply and directly as you can." Good organization of material is essential for creating the greatest impact.

"GARDLINES"

1. Speeches must be structured to an exact plan.
2. Speaking success is not accidental. A successful speech has a starting point and a concluding point, with the material moving in a straight line from one point to the other.
3. The anatomy (three basic parts) of a speech:
   a. The Opener
      (1) Open the listeners' minds—secure undivided attention
      (2) Keep their minds open—a brief preview
   b. The Body
      (1) Present logically arranged major points

      (2) Have each point reinforced with back-up material

   c. The Close

      (1) Make a brief review of topic and major points

      (2) Conclude conclusively

4. You can be very effective in two or three minutes with thought-out material.

5. The first step in making your speech outline is to define and arrange the major points in a logical sequence.

6. The second step is to determine your best, quality reinforcement (back-up) material. It can be in the form of:

   a. Facts

   b. Exhibits

   c. Testimony of other people's experiences

   d. Quotations

   e. Demonstrations

   f. Visual aids

   g. Definitions

   h. Poems

   i. Contrasts

   j. Examples

   k. Analogies

   l. Statistics

   m. Restatements

   n. Question-and-answer periods

   o. Hand-outs

7. Use the proper balance and diversification of good reinforcement material.

8. Determine the opening and closing after the body has been constructed.

9. Openers and closes are so important every word should be well thought out and they should be memorized.

10. All material must be reduced to its simplest form and made to be brief, clear, and specific fitting your exact time slot.

11. It's best to conclude your speech while the audience still wants more.

12. A longer speech doesn't necessarily guarantee it's better. The shorter the talk, the more chance you have of success provided the subject is adequately covered.

THOUGHT-PROVOKING QUOTES

The higher you climb on
the mountain, the harder
the wind blows.
SAM CUMMINGS

Becoming well organized
is a goal seldom reached
in one lifetime.
ARNOLD GLASOW

Ideals are like the stars—
we never reach them, but like
the mariners on the sea, we
chart our course by them.
CARL SCHURZ

Always imitate the behavior
of the winners when you lose.
GEORGE MEREDITH

All men commend patience,
although few are willing
to practice it.
THOMAS A. KEMPIS

Good manners and soft words
have brought many a difficult
thing to pass.
JOHN VABRUGH

Merely ignoring a problem
will not make it go away. . . .
Nor will merely recognizing it.
CULLEN HIGHTOWER

Grow angry slowly—
there's plenty of time.
RALPH WALDO EMERSON

Steady nerves and a quiet
mind are not things we go out
and find; they are things we
create.
JOHN R. MILLER

In any controversy, the
instant we feel anger we
have already ceased striving
for the truth and have begun
striving for ourselves.
THOMAS CARLYLE

Responsibilities gravitate
to the man who can shoulder
them and the power to him
who knows how.
ELBERT HUBBARD

The superior man is firm in
the right way and not merely
firm.
CONFUCIUS

There is nothing in the
world so much admired as
a man who knows how to bear
unhappiness with courage.
SENECA

The measure of a man is the
way he bears up under
misfortune.
PLUTARCH

8

TECHNIQUES TO INFLUENCE THE AUDIENCE

*The primary purpose of the speech
is to communicate and thereby
to influence human behavior.*

LEW SARETT

Four Ways to Deliver Your Talk

HOW TO MAKE AN ACCOMPLISHED
AND ELOQUENT DELIVERY

Four Ways to Deliver Your Talk Using the Material on Your Note Pad

Everything is all set to go. The speech *outline* is complete with the *major points* and *reinforcement* material. You have planned your *opening* and your *closing*. Now you must decide how you are going to get your message across to the audience. What type of delivery will you use?

Here are four methods of delivery:

1. *Partially memorize using no notes.* Memorize your opener, close, and the outline of major points along with one or two words and/or ideas to help you recall your reinforcement material. You would make about 80 percent of your speech relying on your key words or ideas to help you recall and relate your back-up material and present it in a casual, natural conversational way. This method of delivery lets the speaker keep in constant communication with the audience, because he or she doesn't have to keep glancing up and down at notes. This method is one of the most powerful and dynamic ways of delivering a speech because the speaker has full control of the audience.

I caution you not to use this form of delivery until you have fully developed yourself as a confident and seasoned speaker. This delivery is something that every speaker can strive to achieve and a worthy goal to accomplish. There is little doubt that this is the most effective professional delivery there is, *but there is a great amount of risk and hazard in using this technique.* Professionals are skilled people who are before audiences many hours every week and who can think clearly on their feet and have an excellent memory and recall power. If they happen to make a small mistake or fumble a word, they stay calm and no one in the audience ever notices the error. Beginners and those who do not speak in public every day can be thrown off course by an error.

This method of delivery requires a lot of *preparation, prac-*

tice, courage, and *confidence.* It's for the speaker who is speaking very frequently and who keeps his or her speaking skills extremely sharp.

2. *Partially memorize using notes.* This is an excellent method of delivery and one that I recommend for most people. Transfer your notes from your pad to 3 by 5 *cue cards.* Write down enough of your opener, close, major points, and reinforcement material to help you have all the recall power you need to feel confident. Number your cue cards so that everything is in proper order. Your brief ideas and words should be printed in large enough letters so that they can be easily read. Leave adequate space between each line.

You should memorize your opening, close, major points, and a few words or ideas to help you recall your reinforcement material, but using this method you have the complete reassurance and confidence of knowing that your notes are available to you and can be used at any time. You can glance at your notes so that you keep things moving in a planned, logical way. The pressure is off.

With good preparation and practice using your cue cards, you will do an excellent job of communicating with the audience. Don't look at your notes any more than you have to. You'll be relating your reinforcing and back-up material in an easy, conversational, natural style. The cue cards, if needed, will trigger the illustration, example, experience, so that you'll be thinking and speaking in terms of *ideas* and *things* and not just canned words. You'll be delivering your talk just like the method described above except you have the cue cards to use. They are excellent confidence builders and make speakers feel much more secure.

Speaking effectively with cue cards is an art. You will have to work hard and practice glancing at your cue cards, rearranging them as you progress through your talk so that you hold any distracting movements to a minimum. Practice maintaining good eye contact with the audience as much of the time as possible. Never lose sight of the goal all speakers have: to create a favorable rapport with your listeners. The more eye contact you have with the audience, the better. Therefore, the less you look at and refer to your cue cards, the better rapport you will have with your listeners.

3. *Write out and deliver word for word.* If you are in a speaking situation that demands perfection, by all means write out your talk and deliver it word for word. A typical situation would be a new step-by-step medical procedure, reviewing an important contract, making a report on a new law or regulation, reporting or educating your audience on how to program a new computer, or high-level government talks. This type of delivery is only recommended in absolute-must cases. To be effective using this style of delivery takes much practice. Even the seasoned pros find it difficult, and it's quite common for them to fumble a word now and then.

I urge you not to use this form of delivery unless necessary. Why? Speeches that are read word for word are not very interesting. The speaker uses written language instead of conversational, everyday language. Do you write out everything you say throughout the day? Of course not. Very few people can read a speech and make it interesting and captivating. The audience wants you, your personality, and your personal qualities in the message. The listeners do not want just a body reading a written text.

Using this type of delivery will take many, many practice sessions and hard work to put you, (along with your personality and your personal qualities) into the speech. There is no question that a written text provides a safety net and can make a speaker feel more secure knowing that everything to be said is down on paper. It's the good, natural delivery that usually suffers when a speech is read word for word.

4. *Completely memorize the entire talk word for word.* There is a real danger in memorizing a talk word for word. Memorizing a complete talk can court disaster because the speaker sounds artificial and merely recites words, phrases, and sentences. The speaker is usually self-centered instead of being audience-centered. The delivery comes off as being canned and unnatural. Many times the speaker will use canned, forced, and artificial gestures that are completely foreign to his or her personality.

There is no safety net of notes or written text that's going to catch you if you get in trouble by having a mental block or losing your chain of thought. This type of delivery is certainly not for everybody. It's only for those men and women who have had many hours of experience speaking to groups and who have the ability and time to memorize a complete talk and then deliver it with eloquence and natural spirit. If you are going to memorize a speech, allow plenty of practice time and check up on yourself as your are rehearsing to make sure it's *really you* and *your personality* giving the talk.

Of the four delivery methods I have just covered to help you make an accomplished and eloquent delivery, the one that is far best for everyone who reads this book is item two, "Partially memorize using notes." You should know thoroughly how you are going to open and close your talk and know the outline of the logical major points you want to make and be able to bring in your reinforcement material from your brief notes under each major point.

HOW TO PRACTICE

Don't Over- or Under-Practice

If you over-practice, your talk may sound canned and artificial. The real you may not be in it. If you under-practice, you will sound ill-prepared and will not radiate confidence to your audience. It's very difficult to be influential when you aren't confident and feeling at ease. I've heard far more talks that were under-practiced than those that had been over-practiced. Practice until you feel good and in control of yourself and your speech material. You'll soon identify that comfortable feeling after you've completed a few speeches. Remember, *practice builds confidence!*

Practice Mentally, Out Loud, and with Gestures

Use your imagination and see yourself actually giving your speech before a live audience. You can mentally practice your talk just about anywhere between events throughout the day. At some point before you give your talk, get in a room all by yourself and run over your speech out loud, gesturing and placing emphasis on certain key ideas you want to get across.

Practice pausing. Think in terms of ideas and not words. If you are going to use any type of visual aids, practice with those and make sure your speech is well coordinated and that every move looks smooth. Whatever type of speech delivery you are going to use, *get your speech ideas firmly set in your mind.* If you are using cue cards, practice using them or rehearse reading from your speech text.

Practically everyone feels that the first minute or two of a talk is the hardest part of the whole speech. I agree. That's why I recommend that you memorize your opening statements. After a good, successful opener, and once you have made it through the "hardest adjustment period" of your speech, you've set the pace for success all the way through. Since the close is the recap and conclusion of your whole talk, make sure it also is committed to memory. *There is absolutely no shortcut or anything else that will replace mental and oral practice.*

Record Your Talk

You can learn much about yourself by recording your talk as you practice and then acting as your own critic. By listening carefully and analyzing, you'll quickly learn the parts of your speech that were stated well and the parts that need further work. This is an excellent way to make your final preparation. It is also a good check to make sure that your talk is within the time limits. Videotape recordings are very helpful in that you can see as well as hear yourself in action. It's also wise to record some of your actual speeches before audiences and then analyze them so that you grow with every speaking experience.

You Are the Sum Total of Your Preparation and Practice

When you are on the speaker's platform, the spotlight is on you. *You stand alone.* No one can help you. The sum total of your preparation and practice shows up very clearly by what you say, how you say it, what you do, how you do it, and how you look.

HOW TO SELL YOURSELF AND YOUR IDEAS EFFECTIVELY

What Is True Communication?

My definition of true communication is getting yourself and your message across successfully to the audience in your own natural way. The greatest asset you have to transmit a message is your personality and your personal qualities. Getting in front of an audience and not fully capitalizing on them is a serious mistake.

Professor William James said, "Compared to what we ought to be, we are only half awake. We are making use of only a small part of our physical and mental resources. Stating the thing broadly, the human individual thus lives far within his limits. He possesses powers of various sorts which he habitually fails to use."

Stop and think of the various successful actors, actresses, newspeople, and entertainers you see on television. Why are they successful? Because they developed their own abilities in their own, natural way and they do not try to imitate anybody or anything. They know that they must use their own abilities in their own way to the fullest.

Many beginner speakers feel that they have to be told every single gesture, feeling, or expression to use when they are making a speech. In fact, very few beginners would ever think to look inside of themselves for the traits that would make them successful before a group. A common feeling working with beginners is that unless they are forcing themselves to do things differently when they are before a group, they are failing. *That's backwards and that's wrong.* Why should a person be totally different in front of a group of people than he or she would be at home or at the office? If we feel that we must be a different person when making a speech, aren't we really saying that our personality and personal qualities are not good enough the way they are and aren't we really trying to be something we aren't?

Further develop your speaking abilities in your own individual way. You'll sell yourself and your ideas to the audience. As you grow with public speaking, you will destroy some inferiority complex feelings and inhibitions, and will develop more naturalness every time you give a speech. *That's why public speaking is so much more than just public speaking.* Destroying inferior feelings is bound to be most helpful in every phase of life. Henry C. Link said, "Inferiority complexes are seldom more than senseless timidities that rob courage, sap ambition and sap enterprise." *Be proud of yourself.* I'm convinced inhibitions are the commonest cause of ineffectiveness in speakers today.

NINETEEN DELIVERY TECHNIQUES TO MAKE YOU CONFIDENT, INFLUENTIAL, AND EFFECTIVE

Excellent Speakers Seize the Opportunity of the Moment

Every speaking engagement carries with it a great opportunity of the moment. It's a fresh, new challenge. It's exciting to be able to handle and influence any type of audience, to be accepted, and to get your message across. The following platform and delivery techniques will help you to influence the audience favorably and to seize and handle the opportunity of the moment.

1. *Mentally give yourself a short pep talk while being introduced.* You must maintain the right, positive attitude. William James said, "Our belief at the beginning of a doubtful undertaking is the one thing that assures the successful outcome of any venture." Keep doubtful thoughts out of your mind by conditioning your mind for success with a short, positive pep talk. You want to make a good first impression and be ready to meet the challenge. A pep talk will give a speaker spirit, a positive attitude, initiative, enthusiasm, courage, and faith. Pep talks are not to be taken lightly. *You must be up for the occasion.* Walter Dill Scott said, "Success or failure in business is caused more by mental attitude than by mental capacities." So is success or failure in public speaking. Therefore, ensure your success by mentally giving yourself a short, inspiring, positive pep talk while being introduced. Here are some guidelines to follow:

1. It should be ten to twenty seconds in length.
2. It must stress a positive outcome of the challenge you are meeting.
3. It must be realistic.

For example, "I'm enthused and excited about speaking to this group. I've done my homework and I'm well prepared. I've got a good message. I'll capture this group's attention immediately and I'll be successful all the way through my entire talk." As you silently repeat a pep talk to yourself, say it with zip and excitement. Picture yourself succeeding and you *will* succeed.

2. *Approach your speaking position or podium briskly, confidently, and enthusiastically.* You can be sure the audience has been sizing you up before you were being introduced, while you were being introduced, and right now as you make your way and arrive at your speaking position. Therefore, as you walk confidentally and enthusiastically to the podium or your speaking position, mentally give yourself one last, short pep talk and visually see yourself having a tremendously successful experience. This will help you to radiate the right image and to win the confidence of the group immediately. *Confidence is the companion of success.* Confidence begets confidence. Others see you as you see yourself.

3. *Start off professionally.* If you plan to use notes, in a professional and nondistracting way, place them on the podium. Some speakers have asked me if it's okay to leave their notes on the podium just before the meeting starts. I would not recommend that practice, and here's why. I saw it happen once that the emcee, who was working under the stress of an audience, made the introduction and then unconsciously picked up the various papers he had been using to clear the podium for the speaker. Without realizing it, he took the speaker's notes! I'll never forget that incident, and I'm very sure the speaker won't either. The speaker started out with his thank you for the invite, told one joke, and then said, "And now if the emcee will bring back my notes which he took with him when he cleared off the podium, I'll get my speech underway!"

That was certainly an embarrassing situation that didn't have to occur. I suggest that you place your notes or text in a pocket where they can be slipped out very easily. You may want to carry them in your hand making sure they are being held securely so they don't accidentally fall from your grasp. Perhaps you may want to carry them to the podium in a jacketed notepad folder.

You should always check your notes (or text sheet) to make sure that they are in the right order before you walk into the lecture room. The start of your speech is an inappropriate time to find it necessary to rearrange the order of your notes. I've seen it done many times, but don't let it happen to you. Some speakers seem to delight in letting the audience watch them re-adjust their notes. It's very distracting, unprofessional, and usually radiates excessive nervousness and/or a severe ego problem (giving him or her a feeling of importance). The speaker who does that will not win over the audience and may never get his or her speech off the ground. It indicates a lack of preparation and a lack of being an organized person.

If necessary, again in a professional and nondistracting way, adjust the mike *once and for all.* Make sure that it is the only time an adjustment will have to be made. Don't keep playing with it and adjusting it. That's another very annoying thing many speakers do.

Your notes and/or text are in place, your mike is adjusted, and now you are ready to start speaking. Don't rush. Confidently and calmly look out to your audience, *take one or two deep breaths,* wait for the audience noise to quiet down, and you are off!

Starting off correctly is critical. Getting started is the hardest part and that's why it's important to have your lungs filled and a positive mind. You'll very quickly adjust to the "initial audience stress." If you have done a good job of preparing and know exactly how you are going to open your talk, your preparation will carry you through. A critical time like this is not time for self-doubt and negative thinking. Bovee said, "Doubt whom you will, but never yourself." *Think yourself brave and you will be brave.*

You'll gain even more audience confidence if you start your talk without referring to your notes. *A positive attitude, proper preparation, and total command of the subject are the keys.*

4. *Look like you are enjoying yourself.* What's around you is you! If you are having an enjoyable experience making your talk, the audience will have an enjoyable experience also. You'll get back from your audience exactly what you are sending them. The audience can be compared to a mirror, and if you

are wearing a deadpan expression, you'll get the same response from the group.

Thackery said, "Life is a mirror; if you frown at it, it frowns back; if you smile, it returns the greeting." The audience reacts the same way.

5. *Gestures.* If you get nothing from my book but my message on *gesturing*, your time and money will have been well spent. There has been more nonsensical, misleading, harmful information written in books and/or imparted in classrooms about gestures than any other part of public speaking.

In training hundreds of people to speak in public, the second most-asked question is, "What should I do with my hands? Where can I put them? They feel awkward." Sound familiar? (The first most-asked question is "Do you think I can ever learn how to speak confidently in public?")

It is absurd and ridiculous to tell a man or a woman to gesture here, gesture there, with a certain kind of movement. It may be completely foreign and against the grain of a person's inner traits and makeup to follow those instructions. Effective gestures come from the inside of a person.

No two people are exactly the same and no two speakers will gesture in quite the same way. Speakers are not something that can be poured into a mold and that will all come out in an identical way. That's foolish thinking and usually very detrimental.

Have you ever watched a group of three or four children playing? They gesture perfectly and yet no one has ever told them how to gesture. They are doing what comes naturally and that is exactly what you should do with your hands, arms and body . . . just do what comes naturally.

We become extremely self-conscious when we are standing before a group. That's why we ask what to do about our gestures. Do you ask someone how to gesture in your normal, daily activities? Of course you don't. You go at your various activities in your own natural way and the word *gesture* never enters your mind. That's the way it should be in public speaking also. *Get involved with your message, forget yourself, and just do what comes naturally.* It's really that simple. That's the best advice that I can give you, and it works!

What's wrong with letting your hands hang down beside you? Nothing. I encourage you to do that whenever you aren't gesturing. If it feels *right* to you, do it. There's nothing wrong with occasionally placing your hands on the side of the podium or lecturn when you are not gesturing. I suggest, however, that you do not place your hands in the pockets of your pants or make any nervous, distracting movements with them like jingling the change in your pockets, constantly putting your eye glasses on and off, and so on.

Any gesture that comes from any place other than inside of you is false and manufactured. *Natural gesturing is an excellent tool to use in helping to control stage fright.* Gestures have a tendency to loosen up a speaker and to make him or her more relaxed. When a speaker lets himself or herself go physically, he or she will usually set free a great amount of nervous energy and thus feel more composed and confident.

6. *Eye contact.* Don't ignore the audience. Keep good eye contact with your listeners. Good eye contact helps you to communicate with the *whole* audience. Don't be a left-handed speaker who talks more to the people on his or her left side than on the right side. Don't be a right-handed speaker who talks more to his or her listeners on the right side than on the left side.

Make a habit of using good eye contact. It will take practice. Look out to the right side of your audience, then to the middle, then to the left, and then reverse the whole procedure. Also, look to the front row, the middle, and then to the back row, and reverse that procedure. Try to stay in good eye contact with the audience as much of the time as possible, glancing at your notes or text a minimum of time. When you have used good eye contact, members of the *whole* audience will feel that you have included them in your talk. Good eye contact helps to develop a warm, close, and personal feeling between the speaker and the audience.

7. *Word emphasis.* Stress your important words, phrases, and sentences by placing strong emphasis on them. Word emphasis helps to avoid a breakdown in communication and helps to prevent any misunderstanding. *The meaning of a sentence can be changed completely by varying the emphasis on certain words.* Word

emphasis makes your delivery more forceful, accomplished, and dynamic.

You'll be surprised when you are using good natural gestures how you will be properly and automatically hitting some words harder than others. Everyone uses word emphasis in daily conversation. Listen in on a conversation and see how many times word emphasis is used. Listen to the television or a radio station and listen to how the professionals use word emphasis. The secret to effective public speaking has been stated several times in this book and very simply it is: Be natural and use everyday, easy conversational language when before a group. Word emphasis is certainly part of that.

8. *Use a change of voice volume.* Don't put the audience to sleep by being a dull, monotonous, monotone speaker. An excellent tool to use in keeping your audience's interest and to highlight some of your important phrases and sentences is to use a change in your voice volume. I have seen many speakers use this technique with great results. The speaker would be building up some part of the speech to a climax, then lean over the microphone and very softly give the key words or sentence. The audience almost leans over making sure they hear that important line. This is an excellent technique. The same thing is true about talking more loudly at times.

Dr. Roger Bourland is the minister of the First United Methodist Church that my wife and I attend. Roger is a most effective speaker. While he certainly practices to perfection all of the effective speaking skills I have included in this whole book, he uses two of the techniques exceedingly well. I can always tell when Roger is going to make an important point. He will be citing an illustration or example from his text, then calmly and assuredly he pauses, leans over closer to the microphone, and in softer volume gives the key thought or sentence. What an effective speaker and what effective techniques! Needless to say, this is done in his own natural way as are all of the various techniques he uses.

9. *Pauses.* As previously mentioned, the pause helped the softer volume to be even more effective. When coming to important words in your speech, just before you pronounce that key word, use a pause. A pause is very effective in helping to

get certain words or phrases across to the audience. Any time you ask the audience a question, be sure to pause, letting the audience have a couple of seconds to think about the answer to your question.

Pauses, when used effectively, radiate self-confidence out to the audience. A beginner speaker will usually rush through his or her talk, indicating that he or she will be happy when the talk is completed. The professional is going to move the talk right along but is going to periodically and assuredly use a pause effectively to help get his or her message across. *A properly used pause is as effective as a word.*

10. *Stress important phrases or words by speaking slower.* Another excellent technique to use in making certain words or phrases stand out is merely to pause and then slowly state the key words that you want emphasized and then go back to your normal speaking rate. It's a very natural and simple technique, yet it is very effective. You'll find that in your everyday conversations you use this technique automatically and without thinking. Listen in on other people's conversations and you'll determine the frequent use of this effective technique.

For example, say you want to stress and emphasize two words, *truth* and *creation,* in this short statement: "Poetry is simply literature reduced to the essence of its active principle. It is purges of idols of every kind, of realistic illusions, of any conceivable equivocation between the language of (pause—slower) *truth* (back to normal) and the language of (pause—slower) *creation.*" Practice saying that.

In the next example, say you want to stress the words *impatience* and *laziness:* "There are two cardinal sins from which all others spring, (pause—slower) *impatience* and *laziness.*" Then, speed back up to your regular speaking rate starting with the next sentence.

11. *Stand erect and poised.* Always use your best posture by standing tall and proud. Being poised in all types of speaking situations radiates confidence. Don't make a lot of lack-of-confidence movements such as bouncing back and forth on one foot to the other, excessively playing with your eyeglasses, frequently putting you hands in your pockets and taking them back out, playing with your hands in front of you making a

speaker's triangle with your fingers, slouching and excessively leaning on the podium, playing with the mike or cord, or constantly shuffling your notes as if a game of cards was going to be played.

Stand erect and poised, because your posture has a very definite effect upon the audience. Just as sloppy clothing radiates a sloppy speech, a sloppy and unpoised posture radiates a sloppy speech and an insecure speaker.

12. *Speak loudly enough so that everyone can hear.* The audience came to the meeting expecting to hear everything that is taking place. If they can't hear the speaker, the audience will become annoyed very quickly, and rightly so. You must learn to speak loudly enough so that everyone can hear you. It makes no difference as to how small a part of the meeting you feel you have, be it to introduce the guests, give the announcements at the end of the meeting, give the nominating report, or read the minutes of the last meeting, make it a point to arrive in the meeting room a few minutes early and practice talking into the mike. You'll get accustomed to hearing your voice at the right volume level and you'll feel more confident. Adjust the volume if necessary. *Speak confidently into the mike.*

If you are not using a mike, make sure you are talking loudly enough for everyone to hear you clearly in the back of the room. You'll really have to project. In fact, to you it may seem like you are shouting.

Always be prepared to project your voice if the public address system should break down right in the middle of your talk. You'll have to continue without one. I was speaking in Houston one day to four hundred people when halfway through my talk the mike went dead. I was at a critical spot in my talk. I increased my volume and successfully completed my presentation. For twenty-four hours I was so hoarse I could barely speak, but I succeeded in completing my speech. The more experience you get, the more you'll know how much volume the mike should have for you to be clearly heard, or if you aren't using a mike, how much increased volume you will have to use. Obviously, the size of the room and audience will make a big difference. As you become more experienced, you'll know how much volume is the just right amount. While learning and getting more experience, a good rule to follow is to speak with a little more volume than you think is necessary. That little more volume than you think is necessary will probably be the just right amount.

13. *Be humble and audience-centered, not self-centered.* Make it a firm rule never to talk down to your audience. Don't put yourself on a high pedestal with the audience way beneath you. The audience likes a speaker to poke a little fun at him- or herself. Of course, don't humble yourself to the point of losing the audience's confidence, but the listeners like a speaker to admit to a foolish thing he or she did. This shows that you are human, and an audience loves that.

For example, in my sales seminars I tell my audience I doubt that there is a mistake they could make that I haven't already made . . . "Let's see a show of hands, how many of you have done like I have done? I made the sale but, because I didn't stop talking, I actually bought the merchandise back." The hands go up and I begin to see smiles. I cite another example or two and bang, I'm off and running and the group is with me. Why? I've identified with them and they have identified with me. I've now got the audience relaxed, and their minds are open and receptive. I'm not on some kind of pedestal or mountain.

As discussed before, it's always good to mention the name of two or three people in the audience or to let them know that some of their accomplishments are outstanding. A word of caution: If your boss or some other important person is in the audience, don't just speak to or try to impress him or her and forget the rest of the audience. That's a serious mistake. Be audience-centered and speak to everyone present.

Still another technique I use to develop a fast rapport with the listeners is to take the mike out of the holder and continue giving my talk while I walk out in the aisle and get right in the middle of the audience. Listeners love that. The speaker feels close to the audience and the audience feels close to the speaker. This technique helps to break down the "head table and podium barrier" that certainly can exist, especially if the head table or podium is placed with lots of empty space to the front row of chairs or tables.

Many convention planners are now placing the podium off to one side of the head table to help the speaker get closer to the audience and to hold head-table distractions to a minimum while the speaker is talking. This does help the speaker to build an even better rapport with the audience. I realize that there are times when you can't slip out to the audience when you are at the head table. If you are at a podium, try to get out from behind it even if it's just for a short time. Then there is nothing between you and the audience. I continue to get very good vibrations from the listeners.

In sum, forget yourself and think only of your listeners and how you can best communicate with them.

14. *Refer to notes only as necessary.* The fewer glances you must make at your notes, the better. With proper preparation, an occasional glance at your notes should be ample. Every time you look at your notes, you have stopped your eye contact with the audience. Look at your notes just enough, and no more, to help you feel more comfortable and to keep your speech flowing.

There is one definite place to read word for word from your notes. That is when you want to quote an expert, to relay important statistics, or to quote an important passage or document word for word. Reading from your note cards or the actual source adds authority and lets the audience know you are extremely accurate in what you are saying.

15. *Minimize your mistakes.* A man or a woman would do nothing in speaking if he or she waited until it could be done so well that he or she would be guaranteed that a mistake would never be made. Every speaker gives three talks: the one he or she prepared, the one he or she gives, and after the event the one that he or she wishes had been given. We can all look back and say "I made a mistake here," or "I made a mistake there." Did the audience notice it? Probably not, unless we called their attention to it. Don't fuss about minor mistakes and don't call the audience's attention to them unless it is absolutely necessary.

Every speaker, the professional included, fumbles a word now and then. If it's just a word, pros take it very lightly and move directly on with their speech. If it's a phrase that was turned around or a tongue-twister of a word or phrase, the professional will smile about it, say something such as, "I've got a case of friction in my diction," and move right on realizing that an audience knows that a speaker is bound to make a mistake once in a while. After a mistake, the professional usually slows up a bit with the delivery, assuring him- or herself that it won't happen again. The beginner will probably give a lengthy explanation, apologize, look embarrassed or disgusted, get emotionally rattled, and sometimes have a hard time getting back on the right track.

Recognize that mistakes always sound much worse to the speaker than to the audience. Don't create a big fuss over a mistake. If it's minor, pass right over it. If it's a somewhat bigger one, make a short correction, poke some fun at yourself in a short statement, and move right on. Audiences are forgiving.

If you happen to remember something that you left out, either move on and leave it out or try to weave it in so that you maintain continuity in your talk. However, don't mention to the audience that you left it out earlier in your speech. *The audience only knows what you tell them.*

16. *Dress conservatively and immaculately.* Your clothing is as essential to your speaking success as your topic and preparation. *Wear clothing that will command the respect of your listeners.* As a general rule, I suggest you wear authority-type conservative attire. Use your clothing to help you be completely successful with every engagement. You want the audience to remember you favorably. Therefore, you must fully earn the audience's respect.

In this day and age, there is no excuse for not being dressed correctly for each speaking occasion. You can buy books on the subject or you can go to the better clothing stores and ask their advice on proper attire.

Being well-groomed has a definite, positive effect on the speaker as well as on the audience. Being well-groomed and wearing proper clothing builds self-confidence and builds a better self-image. Those qualities certainly make a speaker feel much better on the inside and therefore are bound to make a speaker project him- or herself better. You must build yourself up before you can build up an audience. *Your personal appearance is a reflection of your attitude, and that's where it all starts.*

Other people will see us as we see ourselves, and the image

we create to the audience is exactly the image we hold in our minds. In the case of a poorly dressed speaker, the audience automatically thinks of a poorly prepared speaker. It takes much self-discipline to form good working habits always to do the things necessary to bring about speaking success. Henry Parry Liddon said, "What we do upon some great occasion will probably depend on what we already are; and what we are will be the result of previous years of self-discipline." In sum, *the appearances and actions of men and women are the best interpreters of their thoughts.* Very untidy dress will radiate to the audience a very untidy mind and speech.

17. *Keep your energy level high.* Good athletes follow very strict training rules; thus, they form good training habits. They know that they cannot play their best unless they are fully rested and full of energy. Chamfort said, "A man of intellect without energy added to it is a failure." A speaker without energy is also.

A speaker burns up a great amount of energy giving a speech just as the athlete burns up a large amount of energy playing a ballgame. *Do nothing to dull your energy.* Even the best of clothing and good preparation cannot help a tired body with no energy to give a successful speech.

This is the reason why I will not attend a cocktail party, social event, or any other occasion the night before I speak. I've got to be at my absolute best, and that means I have to be rested.

A man or a woman of intellect tries to use his or her time to the best advantage. A good speaker will try to use his or her time not only to prepare his or her speech properly, but will prepare his or her body so as to be up to peak performance for every speaking occasion. Keep your energy level high.

18. *Hold distractions of distributing handouts (if used) to a minimum.* Your goal as a speaker is win and to hold the attention of the audience by using delivery techniques to influence your listeners favorably. There is a big chance that you might temporarily lose the attention of your group while you are distributing handouts. Distributing handouts during a speech must be done with people moving in the aisles, and listeners are attracted to anything or anybody who moves during a speech.

Stop and think when you've been in an audience and the custodian comes in the meeting to open or close a window, the engineer comes in to check on the air conditioning, or the bellhop brings in a message and gives it to the speaker so that an announcement can be made. What did you do? You automatically looked to the person in motion. The speaker lost your undivided attention. Therefore, you must decide if you really want to use a handout and, if so, when is the most effective time to have it distributed. Depending on the purpose of the handout, consider these times for distribution:

1. Have the handout placed on chairs (or tables if room is set up classroom style) before the session starts. This will give the people something to look at while waiting for the session to start. There will be no delays in your talk while waiting for distribution. The audience will have them ready for use at your exact time. Obviously, if the handout is to be used in connection with the climax of your talk, you would not want it distributed early. That would be disastrous. That would be like giving the punchline of a joke before the story is told. You may not want to distribute handouts before the session starts if you are not the first speaker on the program. The attendees would be looking at your material and not paying full attention to the speaker(s) on the program before you. That wouldn't be in good taste.

2. Have someone distribute the handout at the door of the meeting as the attendees arrive.

3. Have a table set up in the back of the room near the exit so the attendees can pick up the handouts as they leave the meeting room.

4. Have someone distribute the handout out at the door of the meeting room as people leave.

5. Plan carefully to have an adequate number of people distribute handouts at the *exact right time in your speech, making sure distribution time is held to an absolute minimum.* Take into consideration that your listeners will probably be looking at the handout for some time after they receive it. This can be good or it can be bad, depending on your speech and its exact purpose.

6. Hand out material at the time you close your speech. Be extremely careful in handing out material right at the close of your speech if you are being followed by another speaker without a

break. If you are being followed by another speaker without a break, either you or the program chairperson should make an announcement that the material should be placed aside for now and referred to later so that everyone can pay close attention to the next speaker. It is extremely rude and unfair to the following speaker to make such a distribution unless it is properly handled. Remember, the next speaker is trying to seize and hold the attention of the group, and you've made his or her job more difficult by giving the audience something to be looking at and thinking about while the next speaker is speaking.

A handout can be an effective way for a speaker to drive home his or her important point(s), but like anything else, coordinating it with your speech delivery is very important.

19. *Leave the podium wth confidence.* Just as you walked briskly and confidently to the podium when you were introduced, make your exit enhance your image as well. Think, walk, and act like a true professional. Keep radiating that positive attitude. This is no time for a mental letdown. *Keep projecting success!*

HOW TO MEASURE YOUR PROGRESS

Measure Your Progress by the Obstacles You Learn to Overcome

I have told you there can be many obstacles to overcome in achieving your goal of influencing the audience favorably. I have tried to give you every known idea I have to save you time and frustration in being able to influence an audience successfully. I urge you to practice continually the various techniques contained in this chapter as well as in the whole book. Every audience has its own personality, so you must be prepared to handle any type group. Anything worth achieving is worth working hard for and paying the price. There is no feeling in this world that compares with self-reliance, of knowing you can do it. The victory of speaking success is half won when one gains the habit of work. I have stressed this many times, there is no substitute. Hard work of preparaton and practice and learning from every experience builds in just that much more *self-reliance*. The more *self-reliance* you have, the more *natural* your delivery will be. The more *natural* your delivery, the more *effective* you will be in *communicating* with the group.

Booker T. Washington said, "I have learned that success is to be measured not so much by the position that one has reached in life as by the obstacles which he or she has overcome while trying to succeed." Be determined to succeed. Then every obstacle becomes a learning experience. Every learning experience builds even more self-reliance and that builds success. You can do it!

"GARDLINES"

1. There are four ways to deliver your talk using the material on your note pad.
   a. Partially memorize using no notes.
   b. Partially memorize using notes.
   c. Write out and deliver word for word.
   d. Completely memorize the entire talk word for word.
2. You should know (memorize) your opener and your close thoroughly.
3. Practice builds confidence. Don't over-practice or don't under-practice.
4. True communication is successfully getting yourself and your message across to the audience in your own natural way.
5. An excellent speaker is one who seizes the opportunity of the moment.
6. In your own way, use the following delivery techniques to favorably influence the audience.
   a. Mentally give yourself a short pep talk while being introduced.
   b. Approach your speaking position or podium briskly, confidently, and enthusiastically.
   c. Start off professionally.
   d. Look like you are enjoying youself.
   e. Gesture.
   f. Eye contact.
   g. Word emphasis.

   h. Use a change of voice volume.

   i. Pauses.

   j. Stress important phrases or words by speaking slower.

   k. Stand erect and poised.

   l. Speak loudly enough so everyone can hear.

   m. Be humble and audience-centered, not self-centered.

   n. Refer to notes only as needed.

   o. Minimize your mistakes.

   p. Dress conservatively and immaculately.

   q. Keep your energy level high.

   r. Hold distractions of distributing handouts (if used) to a minimum.

   s. Leave the podium with confidence.

7. The surest way not to fail in public speaking is to be determined to succeed.

8. Every obstacle you successfully overcome builds self-reliance.

9. The victory of speaking success is half won when one gains the habit of work.

10. Absolutely nothing replaces preparation and practice.

THOUGHT-PROVOKING QUOTES

Who bravely dares must sometimes risk a fall.
TOBIAS G. SMOLLETT

The individual needs to be in constant struggle with his environment if he is to develop to his highest capacity. Hard conditons of life are indispensable to bringing out the best in human personality.
ALEX CARRELL

Nothing is more humiliating than to see idiots succeed in enterprises we have failed in.
GUSTAVE FLAUBERT

Come, come, my conservative friend, wipe the dew off your spectacles, and see that the world is moving.
ELIZABETH CADY STANTON

One cool judgment is worth a thousand hasty councils.
WOODROW WILSON

You understand human nature when you are never surprised by anything it does.
VERNON HOWARD

Genius has the power of lighting its own fire.
JOHN FOSTER

Manage yourself first and
others will take your orders.
DAVID SEABURY

If you can give your
son only one gift, let
it be enthusiasm.
BRUCE BARTON

A manager develops people.
Through the way he manages
he makes it easy or difficult
for them to develop
themselves. He directs people
or misdirects
them. He brings out what is
in them or he stifles them.
He strengthens their integrity
or he corrupts them. He trains
them to stand upright and
strong, or he deforms them,
whether he knows it or not.
PETER DRUCKER

Then let us all do what is
right, strive with all our
might toward the unattainable,
develop as fully as we can
the gifts God has given us,
and never stop learning.
LUDWIG VON BEETHOVEN

In times like these, it
is helpful to remember
that there have always
been times like these.
PAUL HARVEY

The mold of a man's fortune
is in his own hands.
FRANCIS BACON

Our chief aim in life is
somebody who shall make
us do what we can.
RALPH WALDO EMERSON

9

MAKING AN EFFECTIVE
SPEECH
OF INTRODUCTION

Half the world is composed of people
who have something to say and can't, and the
other half who have nothing to say and keep on saying it.

ROBERT LEE FROST

Effective Introduction Techniques

HOW TO PREPARE THE AUDIENCE
FOR THE SPEAKER

Make Conditions Right for the Speaker's Success

The introducer sets the atmosphere and the pace. A speech of introduction has two vital purposes in order to prepare the audience properly for the speaker. *Every speaker deserves and desires a proper introduction.* Yet, one of the most neglected speeches is the speech of introduction. I have found that 75 percent of the speeches of introduction are ineffective, boring, and/or very incomplete. They do not fulfill the two vital requirements of an introduction speech.

Keep these two requirements in mind when building a speech of introduction:

1. To sell the speaker and his or her qualifications.
2. To sell the topic so that the audience wants to listen.

The introducer has the responsibility of seeing to it that those vital requirements are achieved—no more or no less—thus making the conditions right for the speaker's success. I have stated several times in this book that the speaker must be properly prepared for the audience. It is also critical that the audience must be properly prepared for the speaker.

HOW TO MAKE SECONDS COUNT

In a Speech of Introduction, Every Word Must Count

John Wilson said, "The knowledge of words is the gate of scholarship." Your knowledge of words is the gate to a short, effective speech of introduction. *All weak links must be left out.* All words and phrases must make a *strong* contribution to fulfilling the two basic requirements.

THIRTEEN COMMON PITFALLS TO AVOID

Here is a list of thirteen *"do nots"* that are common reasons why speeches of introduction are ineffective, boring, and/or incomplete.

1. *Don't give the speaker's talk.* Let the speaker make the speech! Many times, the introducer wants to be especially kind to the speaker, so he or she gets carried away and actually starts giving the speaker's talk. That is a real injustice to the speaker. Most of the time when that happens, the introducer, while meaning well, lacks true understanding of the purpose of the introduction. Often, the introducer does this for lack of good preparation and organization.

I'll never forget how one evening I was attending a community meeting and the speaker was to give a twenty-minute talk about his experiences on a recent three-week trip he had taken to Russia. The introducer meant well, I am sure. He spent five minutes introducing the speaker, and in doing so ran through the highlights of the whole trip. The introducer had heard this speaker give this talk in a different community two or three days before.

When the speaker finally got to start his speech, his opening words were, "I feel like the little kid on Christmas day who had opened up all of his packages and the climax was over. He looked to his mother and said, 'Is there anything else for me to do?' After that lengthy introduction, I feel like that little kid—is there anything else for me to do? It's been pretty well said."

Don't be guilty of this common error. *The audience wants to hear the speech from the speaker, not the introducer.*

2. *Don't say, "A speaker who needs no introduction."* Every speaker needs a proper introduction. If he or she doesn't need an introduction, why are you making one? That phrase is completely worn out and trite. That expression distracts from rather than attracts to the introduction. It adds absolutely nothing to the introduction.

3. *Don't make wild claims about the speaker's performance.* The introducer must sell the speaker's qualifications, his or her track record, and the topic and its importance. Stay away from, "He's a super speaker," "She's fantastic," "He'll motivate you,"

"She'll make you laugh," "He's a great speaker," or "She'll leave you inspired." Those are nothing but wild claims. The listeners will judge for themselves how well the speaker can do those things and how good the speaker really is.

An interesting thing happens when the introducer says, "He'll motivate you." There are some people in the audience who will say to themselves, "I don't want to be motivated," or some will say, "Let's just see how he or she can motivate me. I'll not let him. I'll prove him wrong." The same thing is true about, "He'll make you laugh." Some in the audience will say to themselves, "Let's see him do it. I'll bet that guy can't make me laugh." Psychologically, all those words and phrases are bad. You can properly build up a speaker and his or her topic without making wild claims. As I mentioned earlier in this book, the audience is the judge and jury and they'll decide the case for themselves.

4. *Don't make the introduction "too" long.* A good rule to follow is to always try to make a complete speech of introduction in sixty seconds. Never exceed ninety seconds. This keeps the introducer from rambling on and on. Ninety-five percent of the time, sixty seconds is ample. *You must condense your material.* As with any speech, you must be brief, clear, and specific. The audience came to hear the speaker, not the introducer. The introducer can be very effective in sixty seconds. Preparation is the key.

5. *Don't forget the speaker's name and how to pronounce it correctly.* The introducer belittles a speaker when he or she says, "I think that's the way the speaker pronounces his or her name." I've seen some introducers turn to the speaker and say, "That is the way you pronounce it, isn't it?" The introducer better know the name for sure and how to pronounce it correctly. The same thing is true for everything that is in the introduction.

6. *Don't try to be "funny."* Keep your mind on the vital requirements of a speech of introduction. If you are that unique person who can make a humorous one-liner relate and help fulfill the vital requirements of a speech of introduction, go ahead and use it. The odds are very much against you that humor will help your introduction. In fact, trying to use humor will probably turn out to be one of those "weak links." Why?

First, you don't have time. Second, the chances are that your humor will fall flat and won't add a thing to your introduction. It will prove to be distracting rather than attracting. With the odds that I have just cited, why would you want to chance it?

In all of the times that I have been introduced and humor was used as part of the introduction, I have yet to see it really *add* to the introduction. Most of the time, it has ended up with the introducer sitting down saying to him- or herself "I wish I hadn't said that," because the humor failed.

7. *Don't fail to start the applause.* The introducer sets the pace. When the introduction is completed, by all means start the applause. Don't wait for someone else to do it. The audience will follow you and your example. You must get the speaker off to a strong start. Stay at the podium or lecturn until the speaker arrives and *lead the applause enthusiastically.* (Start the applause when the speaker has finished also.)

8. *Don't fail to verify your material.* Nothing is as embarrassing as to have the speaker start his or her talk by correcting some of the statements made by the introducer. All the information should be accurate and current. The surest and best way to handle anything that is questionable is to verify it ahead of time with the speaker. Mistakes such as those can be easily prevented. There's no excuse for a mistake like that.

9. *Don't assume that the audience knows the speaker, his or her qualifications, the topic, and why they should listen.* Never cut short your introduction because of premeeting publicity, mail outs, radio, TV, or newspaper reviews or releases. That serious mistake is made frequently. It can handicap the speaker. Always make a proper speech of introduction regardless of how much premeeting publicity has been used.

To assume that an audience knows all of the pertinent information about the speaker and his or her topic completely ignores the purpose of an introduction. The introducer must make sure that the audience is prepared for the speaker. I can tell you from experience that you've got a problem when the introducer comes off with, "You have all been reading and hearing about our speaker and what he's going to tell us, so without further ado I'll turn the meeting over to him (or her)." Whenever that has happened (even though I've tried to prevent it), the introducer sits down, there is dead silence, and the room is full of highly skeptical people. I have felt like a sheep herder at a cattleman's convention! My job now is to win over the audience in an icy, cold atmosphere. In practically every case when this has happened to me, I've had to spend extra time and lots of extra hard work to get the audience with me. An audience will not accept a speaker until they know how the speaker has earned the right to be in the front of the room talking to them.

Most of the time when this has happened, the introducer had a bad case of audience fright and just said anything to get the introduction over and done with. Never let premeeting publicity influence your speech of introduction. Nothing replaces an effective speech of introduction.

10. *As your final statement presenting the speaker, don't say, "I give you Mr. XXX," or "May I present Mrs. ZZZ."* You can't give the speaker away. You do not have to ask permission to present the speaker because you have been requested to present the speaker, so . . . just do it!

Let's say that you have finished the introduction except for actually presenting the speaker. This should be the climax. Make it short, spirited, snappy, and professional. I suggest these simple phrases: "I present Mr. X," "I introduce Mrs. Z," "Please welcome Mr. X," or "Here's Mrs. Q."

11. *Don't say, "This is what the speaker said I should say."* I'll never understand why introducers think it's funny or cute to be about halfway through their introduction and say something like this, "Gee, this person must really think he or she is good . . . he or she told me to say all this stuff!"

It is rude to the speaker, but it actually happens. Don't be guilty of that.

12. *Don't fail to state the speaker's name two or three times.* One way to make sure that the audience knows the speaker's name is to use it two or three times in your introduction. It should be pronounced correctly, clearly, and distinctly, as well as loudly enough for everyone to hear it. Don't overdo it. I suggest it be used in the opening sentence, somewhere in the body of the introduction, and again right at the end. (See the introduction outline that follows in this chapter.)

There is one exception to this. If you want to build in the element of suspense or surprise, and provided the speaker's name is well-known, it's fine to hold the speaker's name until the very last. You have seen this done many times on television, bringing in a big name at a banquet or convention and at political rallies, and so on. The speaker's name becomes the climax after curiosity has been aroused. To use this technique successfully, the speaker should be well-known. Otherwise, proceed as previously discussed.

13. *Don't bring in your personal views or opinions.* Your job is to make an effective speech of introduction, not to be expressing your views and opinions about the speaker's topic. Yet, I've often heard comments such as, "I take a different view of it than our speaker, but that's okay," or, "I didn't think there was a better way to make the plan work, but maybe the speaker can show us." The audience doesn't care about your personal views and opinions when you are introducing a speaker. Those extra, off-the-cuff remarks, can hurt a speaker's chances of success. When the introducer brings in his or her personal views and opinions, the audience is saying to themselves, "Just introduce the speaker!"

HOW TO GET THE SPEAKER OFF
TO A STRONG START

The following "*do*" list will help you to get your speaker off to a strong, enthusiastic start.

1. *Do be very positive.* If you have a poor attitude about making the speech of introduction, the audience will have a poor attitude also. If you have a positive attitude about the speech of introduction, the audience will also. *The introducer sets the stage for the speaker.*

2. *Do bring in only important speaker and topic related points.* Be well-prepared and organized. Make every word count, and eliminate all nonessential material. *Sift all the appropriate material down and condense it to its most compact form.*

I recently heard a speech of introduction in which the introducer mentioned eighteen points about the speaker's qualifications. The introduction was much too long, boring, and ineffective. When you have many points of qualification to cite, boil them down to four or five of the most important, related points. In the case of degrees, mention the one or two highest degrees. In the case of awards, mention the one or two highest awards—not five, six, or seven. In sum, bring in the significant background points that relate to the speaker's topic, being as brief as possible.

3. *Do be enthusiastic, poised, and confident.* Act and speak with confidence. Be alive and animated! If you are not enthused about making the introduction, you shouldn't make it. Build your speech of introduction to an exciting climax.

4. *Do practice until your introduction is perfected.* Make notes on 3 × 5 cue cards. Practice and practice until you can make the introduction by referring to the cue cards with a minimum of glances. You may want to memorize your introduction and have the cue cards on the lectern in case you feel you need them. Remember, your introduction should be given in a natural, easy conversational way. Don't let it sound artificial and canned. Be dynamic in your own style of delivery.

5. *Do use good eye contact.* Stay in communication with the audience. Don't give your speech of introduction to the speaker. That's a common error.

After you give your last sentence, "Ladies and gentlemen, I present Mr. J. J. Jokes," *insert a brief pause. Now look* to Mr. Jokes, gesture, and say, "Mr. Jokes." That's the only time you should look at the speaker.

6. *Do greet the speaker at the podium.* While leading the applause, as mentioned earlier in this chapter, stay at the podium until the speaker arrives. On the speaker's arrival, give him or her a smile, a welcome gesture, and return to your chair immediately.

7. *Do include yourself, and the head table if there is one, in the speech of introduction.* I recommend you say *"Our* speaker—" instead of *"Your* speaker." When stressing the importance of the topic, say, "This is important to all of *us*—" instead of, "This is important to all of *you*." This simple technique prevents the introducer from talking down to the audience and brings in every person in the room as part of the listeners.

8. *Do be a good listener.* As soon as you complete the intro-

duction and have sat down in your chair, give the speaker your undivided attention. Listen. No whispering. Do nothing to distract any attention away from the speaker.

9. *If assigned, do thank the speaker on closing.* The introducer usually has the responsibility and duty to return to the podium and make a very brief "thank you" immediately following the completion of the talk. If a recap of the speech is made at this time, it should briefly contain one or two highlights of the speech. *One or two sentences are sufficient.* Make the review polished and professional.

THE FIVE-STEP FORMULA FOR MAKING EFFECTIVE INTRODUCTIONS

Use Simplicity and Brevity

Here's some good advice from Luc de Clapiers, "When thought is too weak to be simply expressed, it is clear proof that it should be rejected." Make your speech of introduction simple and reject anything that would make it otherwise. Be brief and try to condense it to sixty seconds or less, never more than ninety seconds. With proper preparation, you'll be very effective in one minute or less!

Here are the five simple steps to make an effective introduction.

1. Speaker's name—one sentence.
2. Speaker's expertise—four or five condensed sentences on qualifications.
3. Speaker's topic—one sentence.
4. Topic's importance to audience—two or three sentences.
5. Present the speaker—one sentence.

An example speech of introduction follows. Let's say the audience is made up of maintenance engineers:

1. Our keynote speaker this morning is Mr. John J. Jones.
2. He (or our speaker) is president of the company he founded in 1946.

In 1948, he developed, patented, and since then has successfully sold his "Kustom Kleaner" machine, not only in the United States but in nineteen foreign countries, updating it annually with the latest innovations.

He holds a Ph.D. degree in Mechanical Engineering from Northwestern University.

In May of this year the United States Chamber of Commerce presented him with the highest award possible, the "National Outstanding Business Person of the Year," for his contributions toward helping industry and institutions keep their buildings clean.

He is author of the best-selling book, *You Can Keep It Clean.*

3. Mr. Jones is well-qualified to speak on the subject, "What to look for when purchasing cleaning equipment."

4. His topic is of real importance to every one of us, because we all want our dollars invested in equipment that pay the maximum benefits, and we want our buildings to be spic and span to create a favorable image to our customers.

5. "Ladies and gentlemen, I present Mr. John J. Jones." Turn and face Mr. Jones, gesture, and say, "Mr. Jones." Start the applause.

SIMPLICITY AND WELL-CHOSEN WORDS MAKE FOR SUCCESS

Avoid Weak Links in Your Speech of Introduction

If you have been asked to be an introducer, take the assignment seriously and be very sure that there are no weak links or fuzzy words included. You must look at this speech as vitally important even though it is short. I've seen great programs made even greater by having a strong introducer.

An introduction should be simple, yet it is a neglected part of public speaking. Henry Wadsworth Longfellow said, "In character, in manners, in style, in all things, the supreme excellence is simplicity." Choose your simple words carefully and make every word count. An effective speech of introduction is one that sells the speaker, his or her expertise, and the topic's importance *simply* and *precisely*. When that is accomplished, the person you are introducing will be most grateful because you got him or her off to a splendid start!

"GARDLINES"

1. Every speaker deserves and desires a proper introduction.
2. You must properly prepare the audience for the speaker.
3. A speech of introduction must:
   a. Sell the speaker and his or her qualifications.
   b. Sell the topic and why the audience should listen.
4. Every word in a speech of introduction must count.
5. The thirteen *"do nots"* that render introductions ineffective, boring, and/or incomplete are:
   a. Don't give the speaker's talk.
   b. Don't say, "A speaker who needs no introduction."
   c. Don't make wild claims about the speaker's performance.
   d. Don't make the introduction "too" long.
   e. Don't forget the speaker's name and how to pronounce it correctly.
   f. Don't try to be "funny."
   g. Don't fail to start the applause.
   h. Don't fail to verify your material.
   i. Don't assume that the audience knows the speaker, his or her qualifications, the topic, and why they should listen.
   j. As your final statement in presenting the speaker, don't say, "I give you, Mr. XXX," or "May I present Mrs. ZZZ."
   k. Don't say, "This is what the speaker said I should say."
   l. Don't fail to state the speaker's name two or three times.
   m. Don't bring in your personal views or opinions.
6. Here are nine things to *"do"*:
   a. Do be very positive.
   b. Do bring in only important speaker and topic related points.
   c. Do be enthusiastic, poised, and confident.
   d. Do practice until your introduction is perfected.
   e. Do use good eye contact.
   f. Do greet the speaker at the podium.
   g. Do include yourself, and the head table if there is one, in the speech of introduction.
   h. Do be a good listener.
   i. Do thank the speaker.
7. The five simple steps to make an effective introduction are:

    a. Speaker's name—one sentence.

    b. Speaker's expertise—four or five condensed sentences on qualifications.

    c. Speaker's topic—one sentence.

    d. Topic's importance to audience—two to three sentences.

    e. Present the speaker—one sentence.

8. Simplicity and well-chosen words will make for your success.

9. Everything used in the introduction speech should be essential and accurately stated.

THOUGHT-PROVOKING QUOTES

If you have the will to win, you have achieved half your success; if you don't, you have achieved half your failure.
DAVID V.A. AMBROSE

To do anything in the world worth doing, we must not stand back shivering and thinking of the cold and danger, but jump in, and scramble through as well as we can.
SYDNEY SMITH

All that a man achieves and all that he fails to achieve is the direct result of his own thoughts.
JAMES ALLEN

When you're afraid, keep your mind on what you have to do. And if you have been thoroughly prepared, you will not be afraid.
DALE CARNEGIE

What we see depends mainly on what we look for.
JOHN LUBBOCK

Character is a by-product; it is produced in the great manufacture of daily duty.
WOODROW WILSON

There is nothing so easy but that it becomes difficult when you do it with reluctance.
TERENCE

Too many people are thinking of security instead of opportunity. They seem more afraid of life than death.
JAMES F. BYRNES

If you play it safe in life, you've decided that you don't want to grow anymore.
SHIRLEY HUFSTEDLER

Worry often gives a small thing a big shadow.
SWEDISH PROVERB

What a man knows should find expression in what he does. The chief value of superior knowledge is that it leads to a performing manhood.
CHRISTIAN BOVEE

You can't have a better tomorrow if you are thinking about yesterday all the time.
CHARLES F. KETTERING

The world is full of willing people, some willing to work, the rest willing to let them.
ROBERT FROST

Most of the shadows of this life are caused by standing in our own sunshine.
HENRY WARD BEECHER

10

HOW TO MAKE A MEMORABLE AWARD PRESENTATION

*Speeches cannot be made
long enough for the speakers, nor
short enough for the hearers.*

JAMES PERRY

Make the Award a Moment of Glory

HOW TO MAKE THE HONOREE FEEL
GENUINELY HONORED

The Presentee Must Leave the Meeting
with Pleasant Memories

The presenter has a tremendous amount of responsibility in making an award presentation. The art of properly presenting an award is another neglected part of public speaking. It is taken far too lightly and all too often the presenter does not do a professional job. The presentation comes off as being insincere and full of exaggerated flattery.

This is the recipient's moment of glory. To accomplish this, the presenter must put the spotlight on the honoree and do it *honestly, sincerely, and from the heart.* If this weren't a special occasion, the award would be presented through the U.S. mail or on a one-to-one basis where the presenter and the presentee would agree to meet for a few minutes. It could be at the recipient's house, while on the job, or perhaps while taking a short coffeebreak. *Nothing should be done to in any way dampen the honored feeling the honoree must have while and after being presented his or her award.* You, the presenter, want the honoree to leave the meeting with pleasant memories of a special, unique, genuine, spirited session.

SEVEN GUIDELINES TO MAKE A MEMORABLE
PRESENTATION

Here are some guidelines of things to do, and things not to do, to help you make an award presentation that sparkles, is gracious, and is very memorable.

1. *Place a great amount of importance on the speech, the award, and the honoree.* If you don't, the audience and the honoree won't either. We are living in a day and age when many awards are being presented for many different reasons. Since awards are so common and we see and hear about so many of them being given out, it is quite easy to develop a lackadaisical attitude about awards and their true meaning. I've often seen it

happen that it seemed as if the presenter had the attitude, "Just some more old common everyday awards to give out . . . so what . . . no big deal!"

The presenter's positive attitude is so important. Presenting an award should be made *something extra special,* not looked upon as convention or meeting *"filler time"* or *"not just something that has to be done."* Attitude will not be a problem when you keep your mind on the prime importance the recipient is placing on this event.

2. *Limit your presenter's talk to two minutes or less.* The thing that I have stressed throughout this whole book applies here as well. Be brief, clear, and specific. You often can give a complete presentation speech in less than two minutes. This, of course, would depend on the circumstances and the type of award you are presenting.

The biggest common error I have observed in making this type of speech is when the presenter, in making the recipient feel honored and important, rambles on and on and goes overboard trying to bring in much too much, poorly worded, trite material that finally comes out as cheap and insincere flattery.

I know this is the time for making the recipient feel important and that the presenter wants to be complimentary, but regardless of how good *praise* is, too much of anything is too much. It becomes oversell and/or overkill. The key is to use just enough, and no more, sincere, complimentary achievement remarks. You must be articulate and expressive using well-chosen, descriptive words. As with any talk, this speech must be well thought out, prepared, and organized. Every word must count. Some people can say more in two minutes than others can say in two hours. *The quality of the speech is vital.* You must sort out and bring in relevant, worthy material. As Shakespeare said, "Let thy speech be short, comprehending much in few words."

Outline your important points on 3 × 5 cue cards, making sure you don't overlook any important facts. This is not the time to mix in some of your own ideas, views, and opinions. Practice and practice until your talk flows smoothly and naturally and you are glancing at your cue cards as little as possible.

3. *Deliver your award presentation speech with poise, confidence, and appropriate animation and enthusiasm.* Be very poised and

confident in your delivery. This makes for a more forceful and dynamic presentation.

Also, animation and enthusiasm add tremendously to the pleasant memories of the event. These things all add to this very special moment for the recipient and help to make the presentee the hero!

4. *Use good eye contact with the whole audience.* Except for the very short periods of time when you are glancing at your cue cards, picking up and putting back down the award, and/or when you are reading the inscribed words on the award, stay in good communication with the audience. *Don't talk to the award.*

And don't play with or fumble awkwardly around the award all through your presentation. The award and the unnecessary movements become distracting.

5. *Balance the spotlight on the meaning of the award and the honoree's achievements.* Some award presentations are ineffective because the presenter spends 90 percent of the time building up the award and actually says very little about the person who has earned the award. On the other hand, some presenters are ineffective because they spend 90 percent of the time building up the recipient and very little time is spent to build up the true meaning of the award. The two go hand-in-hand and should be properly balanced out.

6. *Use humor only if it's appropriate and if you have the unique ability.* As mentioned before, trying to be the humorous speaker is standing on thin ice for most people. Use humor only if it's appropriate, and only then if you are one of few people who can get the right response from the audience to make humor effective.

I would classify winning a fish or wildlife award, the barbequer or an athletic award, as being presented at a meeting where things are run on the "light" side. Humor could be very appropriate there, *but then only if* the award presenter has the talent and ability to use humor successfully.

In making award presentations for production, safety, sales, academic, retirement, outstanding accomplishment, service, dealer of the year, business woman of the year, and so on, I would not take any chances on doing anything that could possibly dampen the spirits of the occasion.

A good rule to follow is: If there is any doubt at all about whether or not humor is appropriate and/or the presenter has the ability to use it favorably, by all means do not use it.

7. *If the award fails to arrive in time, do not let the honoree leave the platform with a letdown feeling and nothing in his or her hands.* With proper planning, the situation will never exist where the award fails to arrive in time for the actual presentation. It does happen all too frequently, however. Therefore, it's worthy of a comment.

If the award has not arrived, your first goal is to see to it that the honoree doesn't leave the platform with a depressed, let-down feeling. Don't let him or her leave with nothing in hand.

I know it is bad to apologize, but in this case it is justified. Make a brief explanation to the audience and the presentee as to why the real award is not present. The next thing to the actual award is to present the recipient with a well-typed "letter of certificate" in which it is certified that the recipient has earned the award. The same words inscribed on the award often can be put in this letter. Make sure that the letter bears a signature from the proper party. Place the "letter of certificate" in a proper size envelope, or better yet, make a trip to a nearby store and purchase a frame. You can frame the letter and use it for the presentation, stating that the real award will be delivered promptly to the recipient on arrival. This prevents the honoree from leaving the front of the room with nothing to show for his or her accomplishment. Even though you had to apologize, your job as the presenter is to keep the program moving in a positive, spirited atmosphere.

HOW TO BUILD THE PRESENTATION TO A PERFECT CLIMAX

The Manner of Presentation Is Equally as Important as the Award

Johann Kaspar Lavater said, "A gift, its kind, its value, and appearance; the silence or pomp that attends it; the style in which it reaches you, may decide the dignity or vulgarity of the giver." I cannot stress too strongly the importance of the style and manner in which an award reaches the recipient. An ineffective presenter can and usually does make a major award appear to be a small, minor award. A good presenter can and does make a small, minor award appear to be an important, major award.

Here's a simple four-step format to use as an outline for making an effective award presentation. Naturally, you'll have to be flexible and tailor each presentation to fit different types of awards and different occasions, but the basic outline will work for all presentations.

1. *Announce the award you are presenting.* Pick up the award and immediately announce the name of the award you are presenting by reading from the inscribed title. Very briefly show it to the audience (unless for some good reason you feel showing it to the audience at this time would not be appropriate . . . perhaps you want to show the award as the climax right at the end) and place it back down on the table. While holding the award, talk to the audience and not to the award. Hold it high enough so all can see it, and hold it off to your left or right so that it doesn't hide your face. Display and handle the award with professionalism and pride. Be an example of a positive, spirited person.

2. *Why this award?* Tell the audience why this award is being presented, why it's important, and what the requirements are to earn the award. Give some history of the award. Is this an annual award? Tell the first year it was presented and why the award has been continued. Give two or three brief remarks about the background of the company or organization. If this is a special award, tell why it was decided to give the award and why it is important.

3. *Why this recipient?* On what basis was this person selected to receive the award? Give the specifics. How was this person qualified? Who selected this person? What contribution has this person made? What was outstanding about his or her work and the success he or she has enjoyed? Cite two or three actual examples and illustrations from the recipient's background.

4. *Present the award to the recipient.* Pick up the award, if possible, hold it in your left hand so that you can congratulate the recipient with your right hand. If there is any other part of the inscribed wording you want the audience to hear, read it now. Enthusiastically make the actual, brief presentation. Build it to a climax, holding the recipient's name until the end. Start the ap-

plause and ask the recipient to come forward to receive the award. If proper and desired, ask the award winner to say a few words.

This four-step outline will enable you to do a commendable job of making any award presenting speech you may be called upon to make. Due to the many varieties of awards and occasions, you will have to be versatile and tailor the material under each of the four points to fit your exact, specific event. Here's an example:

1. (Pick up award) Tonight, I'm presenting this outstanding, beautiful award inscribed (read from award) "National Top Producer—19XX" to an outstanding sales person who has really made things happen and kept things moving. (Display award to audience and quickly put it down on table.)

2. This highest award of achievement that our company can bestow upon any salesperson was started in 1955, the year we started business. This is an annual award and it goes to the person who by verified sales records, has produced the most dollar volume in the past calender year. Everyone is qualified to win this award and there is no limit to the number of times it can be won. Mr. Doe, our president, and all of the officers and workers are most grateful to the recipient because it's only through sales that we can stay in business and keep growing.

3. Our recipient is an outstanding example of how to turn adversities into achievements. This salesperson always displays a positive mental attitude and is one who believes when the going gets tough, the tough get going. This salesperson lost the largest account in the assigned territory because a fire completely destroyed the customer's business. This salesperson worked hard and has now developed a new customer who is doing even more business with us than the one who was lost. This honored salesperson lost four weeks of work while in the hospital, and still wasn't stopped from maximum production. This salesperson proves it's not the years in the business that determine a person's success. It's how a person handles the job that determines the success. This salesperson, only with us three years, handled the job so well last year that a record high dollar volume of $15,500,000.00 in new business was written, an exciting and impressive amount.

4. (Pick up the award and if possible, hold it in your left hand.) Ladies and gentlemen, it's an honor to present this "National Top Producer—19XX" award, which also has inscribed the words, "A True Champion Closer," to (pause) Mr. Jeff J. Jones!! (Start the applause and ask Mr. Jones to come forward.) Present the award to him with your left hand while congratulating him with your right hand. If you desire, ask the recipient to say a few words of acceptance.

This very simple four step formula will work for any type of award you might be presenting. The key to using it successfully is to be flexible and tailor your material. As with any speaking task, preparation and practice make for success.

If you are presenting fifteen similar awards to the Boy Scouts, by tailoring you could go through steps one, two and three and then use step four for each boy as he comes forward. The second option is to go all four steps reading all the names of recipients and then present all at one time.

Does the recipient's name have to be kept until the end? Certainly if you have been building up suspense and the name has been a secret. The name of the recipient should be the climax to the whole presentation. Even if the recipient has been announced prior to the presentation, I still recommend that the name be last and that you build your award speech to a real climax.

IT'S WHAT THE RECIPIENT TAKES HOME THAT REALLY COUNTS

Presenting an Award Should Be a Pleasure and an Honor

John Tillotson said, "There is little pleasure in the world that is true and sincere beside the pleasure of doing our duty and doing good. I am sure no other is comparable to this." When you have sent the award winner home with pleasant memories and the feeling of being proud of his or her accomplishment, you know you have done your duty well. Remember, the manner in which the award is presented, the words and the spirit, are just as important, maybe even more so, as the award itself. The important thing about the award presentation is the recipient. Let this truly and sincerely be the recipient's *"moment of glory!"*

"GARDLINES"

1. The presentee must leave the meeting with pleasant memories and saying to himself or herself, "I'm really proud of me."
2. The presenting speech should be unique, genuine, spirited and memorable.
3. Some general guidelines to make an effective presenting speech are:
    a. Place a great amount of importance on the speech, the award, and the honoree.
    b. Limit your presenter's talk to two minutes or less.
    c. Deliver your award presentation speech with poise, confidence and appropriate animation and enthusiasm.
    d. Use good eye contact with the whole audience.
    e. Balance the spotlight on the meaning of the award and the honoree's achievements.
    f. Use humor only if it's appropriate and if you have the ability.
    g. If the award fails to arrive in time, do not let the honoree leave the platform with a let-down feeling and nothing in his or her hand.
4. The four step format for making an effective, climactic award presentation speech is:
    a. Announce the award you are presenting.
    b. Why this award?
    c. Why this recipient?
    d. Present the award to the recipient.
5. Presenting the award should be a real pleasure and an honor.
6. It's what the recipient takes home that really counts.
7. Let this truly and sincerely be the recipient's "moment of glory!"

THOUGHT-PROVOKING QUOTES

The right man is the
one who seizes the moment.
GOETHE

The best way to know a man
is to watch him when he is
angry.
HEBREW PROVERB

Every production of genius
must be the production of
enthusiasm.
BENJAMIN DISRAELI

Build broken walls and
make every stone count.
JOHN BROWN

He that climbs a ladder
must begin at the first rung.
WALTER SCOTT

No man ever distinguished
himself who could not
bear to be laughed at.
MARIA EDGEWORTH

How far you go in life
depends on your being tender
with the young, compassionate
with the aged, sympathetic
with the striving, and tolerant
of the weak and strong.
Because someday in your life
you will have been all of these.
GEORGE WASHINGTON CARVER

He isn't a real boss until
he has trained subordinates
to shoulder most of his
responsibilities.
WILLIAM FEATHER

Only he deserves power who
every day justifies it.
DAG HAMMARSKJÖLD

It is better to plan
less and do more.
WILLIAM ELLERY CHANNING

Most of those who keep
on making fresh starts
make rotten progress.
SHRAGA SILVERSTEIN

A thought for each day: Make
it through until tomorrow.
ROBERT HALF

The good that is in
you is the good that
you do for others.
ROGER BABSON

Half of the world is on the
wrong scent in the pursuit of
happiness. They think it
consists in having and getting,
and in being served by others.
It consists in giving and
in serving others.
HENRY DRUMMOND

11

HOW TO MAKE A GRACIOUS AWARD ACCEPTANCE SPEECH

*Never rise to speak until
you have something to say; and
when you have said it, cease.*

JOHN WITHERSPOON

Successful Techniques for Accepting Awards

HOW TO AVOID BORING YOUR LISTENERS

Stop When You Have Said Enough

As the old expression goes, "When you're done pumping, for goodness sake let loose of the handle." It's much better to say too few words than to bore the listeners with far too many. How much is enough when you are making an acceptance speech? Probably a lot less than you are thinking. In a good many cases, two words will handle the acceptance speech quite nicely: thank you. Many times, that is all that's needed and appropriate. Sir Winston Churchill gave us some good advice when he said, "Short words are best and the old words when short are best of all." Yet, there are so many people who feel that they haven't given justice to the occasion unless they deliver a lengthy, boring, hearts and flowers, much too detailed, ceremonial talk of some kind. Award winners have seen so many other award winners give their talks like that, they feel they must give theirs that way also. They imitate and try to follow bad examples.

That's the first of two reasons why the acceptance speech is mishandled. Because people aren't recipients very often, award winners don't take the steps necessary to obtain effective know-how and a track to run on. Before a group they appear to be grasping for something to say so that they can fill a self-imposed, minimum amount, time slot. So while grasping for something to say and feeling compelled to keep talking, I've seen award winners talk and talk and talk, thank and thank and thank, until the members of the audience are saying to themselves, "Why doesn't he or she shut up and sit down! I wish he or she wouldn't have won the darn thing." I've seen other award winners try to be the funny person and fail miserably and be a complete flop. I've seen some award winners come off with a great, overkill oration (some speaking impromptu and others prepared), putting themselves on a high pedestal and failing to make a favorable impact.

I'm sure most of these award winners had good intentions. They certainly didn't intentionally bomb. For lack of proper know-how, they were following advice of someone who was not qualified and competent or else they unknowingly were following ineffective, wrong examples set by others.

The second reason acceptance speeches fail to go over with maximum impact is that many recipients don't realize how much is enough. They honestly feel that more is better and that's not necessarily true. They forget that when you are done pumping, let loose of the handle. When you have said it, cease! Avoid boring the listeners.

HOW TO BE GRACIOUS AND EFFECTIVE IN THIRTY SECONDS

When you are going to accept an award, seriously ask yourself, is "thank you" enough. When you reason it out, in many cases it is. Sure there will be some occasions where you feel "thank you" is not sufficient for the occasion, so I'm providing you with a very simple four-step formula to help you to do a commendable job of making an acceptance speech when "thank you" isn't enough. This speech should never exceed thirty seconds. You can be very effective in that time limit. Only if you are in an extremely formal atmosphere would you ever consider going longer than that, and even then, make it as short as possible.

1. One sentence: Express your *sincere* gratitude.
2. Two or three sentences: Acknowledge and show appreciation to contributors.
3. One or two sentences: What will you do with award?
4. Two words: Thank you.

You will, of course, have to tailor it for your specific occasion. By following this outline, you will always do a good job. Here's an example acceptance talk:

1. This occasion is very important to me, and I'm honored and grateful to be presented this award.
2. I'm also very grateful and thank those who made outstanding

contributions and supported me. Many extra hours were spent working with me to get this project completed right on schedule. This accomplishment represents a great team effort.

3. I will place this award in my office where it will be displayed with great pride because it symbolizes "people loyalty."

4. Thank you.

In sum, "thank you" or the foregoing simple four-step formula is all you will ever need to be effective accepting your award. The audience is not expecting, and really doesn't want, a lengthy formal acceptance speech. Do your audience, and yourself, a favor. Keep it genuine, simple, and as short as possible.

"GARDLINES"

1. Make it a firm rule that when you are done pumping, for goodness sake let loose of the handle and avoid boring your listeners.

2. Don't feel compelled to make a lengthy acceptance speech.

3. Realize that "more" is not always "better."

4. Sometimes an excellent acceptance speech consists of "thank you."

5. When *thank you* isn't enough, use these simple, four steps:

   a. One sentences: Express your *sincere gratitude*.

   b. Two or three sentences: Acknowledge and show appreciation to contributors.

   c. One or two sentences: What will you do with the award?

   d. Two words: Thank you.

6. Keep your acceptance speech genuine, simple, and as short as possible, never exceeding thirty seconds.

THOUGHT-PROVOKING QUOTES

The past always looks better than it was. It is only pleasant because it isn't here.
FINLEY PETER DUNNE

True success is overcoming the fear of being unsuccessful.
PAUL SWEENEY

I believe that every human
mind feels pleasure in doing
good to another.
THOMAS JEFFERSON

A day of worry is
more exhausting than
a day of work.
JOHN LUBBOCK

To think we are able is almost
to be so, to determine upon
attainment is frequently
attainment itself.
SAMUEL SMILES

While we stop to think, we
often miss our opportunity.
PUBLILIUS SYRUS

Every man can transform the
world from one of monotomy
and drabness to one of
excitement and adventure.
IRVING WALLACE

No man ever sank under the
burdens of the day. It is
when tomorrow's burdens are
added to the burdens of today
that the weight of them is
more than a man can bear.
GEORGE MCDONALD

I like a person who knows
his own mind and sticks to
it; who sees at once what,
in given circumstances, is
to be done and then does it.
WILLIAM HAZLITT

Do not wait for
extraordinary circumstances
to do good actions; try
to use ordinary circumstances.
JEAN PAUL RICHTER

You can never ride on the
wave that went out yesterday.
JOHN WANAMAKER

Why wish for the privilege of
living your past life again? You
begin a new one every
morning.
ROBERT QUILLEN

Every new opinion, at its
starting, is precisely a
minority of one.
THOMAS CARLYLE

When one door closes, another
opens; but we often look so
long and so regretfully upon
the closed door that we do
not see the one which has
opened for us.
ALEXANDER GRAHAM BELL

12

THE SECRET OF SPEAKING IMPROMPTU

A good speech is a good thing,
but the verdict is the thing.

Daniel O'Connell

Successful Impromptu Speaking

HOW TO RELAX AND AVOID PANIC

You Can Do It—There's Nothing to It

You are prepared right now to speak impromptu on a number of topics!! The secret is you must be on the right subject. When you are on the right subject, you can do it. There's nothing to it. You can learn to think and speak on your feet as well as you can on your seat.

Many people hear the word *impromptu* and their panic button has been depressed and all of the alarms go off. Relax immediately. The odds are one to a thousand that you will ever be asked to speak impromptu on an unfamiliar subject. It just doesn't happen.

Let's say you are attending a conference and the chairperson approaches you and says something like this, "We have just been advised that one of our speakers can not be present because of an acute illness . . . will you fill in?"

Or let's say, you are at a meeting and are sitting out in the audience taking in the various speakers and during the coffee break the chairperson asks you to say a few words about your views and feelings on the "topic of the day," which has been discussed by several other speakers.

Or let's say you are at a conference and you disagree with the thinking of the other speakers who have presented their ideas. You have found other ideas to be far more effective. During the coffee break you ask the chairperson for a few minutes to express you findings, or maybe you must jump up and ask the chairperson for time to express your viewpoint right while the meeting is in session.

First, you would not have been asked to express yourself, or you wouldn't have asked permission to express yourself, unless you had knowledge on the subject!

The secret to successful impromptu speaking is to speak on *specific* illustrations, experiences, and examples from your past that you are fully knowledgeable on, either by experience or through past study, and that you have a desire to have other people know about. That's the easiest and most effective way to speak impromptu. When handling impromptu speaking using this technique, you'll find you can think as well on your feet as you can on your seat! You can relax and avoid panic.

THINKING CLEARLY AND SPEAKING EFFECTIVELY ON YOUR FEET

How to Sound Competent, Eloquent, and Polished

The following list gives some proven techniques to help you do a very accomplished job of speaking impromptu, of thinking clearly and speaking effectively on your feet. These points will help you to feel more confident and to help you to be even more influential. Thus, you'll gain more important recognition, further enhance your image, and earn the respect of your listeners. You'll appear competent, eloquent, and polished.

1. *Quickly define your viewpoint, or determine the purpose of your speech.* Stay calm, cool, and collected. Apply the *STOP* formula (*Stop, Think Or Perish!*). If the chairperson, just prior to the start of the meeting or during the break, should ask you to express your viewpoint, request that you be given a few minutes to gather and logically arrange your thoughts. Even if in the middle of the meeting the chairperson looks at you and asks you to say something concerning the topic, again, request a few minutes to formulate your talk. Your request is certainly not out of line, and the audience will understand. If it's a case in which you are in the audience and you want to express yourself, you've had time to be thinking and planning what you are going to say before your request is made.

The first thing for you to do is get your goal clearly in mind by defining your viewpoint and/or your exact speech purpose. *Be definite.* Everything will hinge on this. This stops drifting and rambling. This enables you to collect your thoughts, to think objectively, and to bring in your best backup and reinforcement material. This gives you a starting point and a closing point. This helps to keep you thinking on your feet and talking in an organized way. If you don't know where you are headed, any road will take you there. Know where you are headed and take a straight road to your destination. Before you say one word, you must have it clearly in mind what you want to accomplish. If you have time, make a note of this.

2. *Now choose a specific illustration, experience, or example.* Once you know your definite purpose and/or have clearly defined your viewpoint, the next thing to do is to get quickly in mind from your past, a *specific* illustration, experience or example that will backup and reinforce your speech purpose. You are the authority on *specifics* from your professional or personal life, either from experience or through study.

Choosing your impromptu speech material in this manner will give you additional courage and confidence because you are really prepared. You are the expert on specifics that have happened to you. You'll be talking specifics in your field of expertise. You'll be able to speak on these specifics very well because you have been thinking about them, and no doubt have gone over them and talked about them several times in your life. Louis Calhern said, "Any talk without an explicit example is weak." If you have time, jot down some brief notes of things to include on your 3 × 5 card.

Speaking on specifics makes you persuasive. It helps to eliminate the dilly-dally and arguing that goes on in meetings. Why? Your talk will be clear and convincing. Most of the other attendees will get up and throw out a lot of hot air consisting of wild, exaggerated claims. Your talk will be factual and convincing. It will also be believable. Just tell the group *when* this *specific* illustration, example, or experience happened, *why* it happened, *where* it happened, *what* caused it to happen, *who* was involved, and *how* it happened. When, why, where, what, who, and how are referred to as the six honest serving men. I quote Kipling's short poem:

> I keep six honest serving men
> They taught me all I know
> Their names are WHAT and WHY and WHEN
> And HOW and WHERE and WHO.

When you answer the six honest serving men, you'll be

bringing in enough *specifics* to make your talk captivating, complete, and interesting. You will be speaking impromptu in a very masterful and accomplished way. Don't overlook the dynamic power of *specificity!*

3. *Start strong.* Use any opener mentioned before in this book. You could open with your viewpoint, "My viewpoint is . . . and here's why . . . (specific backup material)," or, "My experience shows it's best to . . . because . . . (specific reinforcement material).

4. *Don't try to cover too much ground.* Many impromptu speeches fail because the speaker hops around going from this point to that point and doesn't adequately cover any point. You'll never be guilty of that PROVIDED you keep your mind on the one definite, exact purpose of your speech. All of your back-up and reinforcement material will be important and meaningful and make a maximum contribution to your overall speech achievement.

5. *Don't apologize anytime.* The audience will know that you are speaking impromptu. The chairperson should by all means announce this. If you jump up on the spur of the moment, it's perfectly obvious to everyone that you are speaking on the spur of the moment. The audience will not be expecting a keynote address.

If you feel that you cannot bring the audience something worthwhile, decline the invitation. Providing a lot of excuses and wasting the audience's time with weak, meaningless material does only one thing . . . it weakens you and everything you have to say. You and your words will be received in a negative rather than a strong, positive way.

6. *Conclude conclusively.* Any closing technique I mentioned earlier would be excellent to use. Be specific. No rambling or fuzzy words. *Close strongly.* For impromptu speaking, the simplest way to close is merely to summarize by stating or restating your overall speech purpose to the audience. Another simple technique for an adequate close is to tell the audience what this specific illustration, example, or experience has proven to you, "From this experience I have learned . . . (be specific)."

When you have given your close, return to your chair immediately. I've seen it happen many times when the impromptu speakers are done that they act as if they don't know what to do. Perhaps they are waiting for someone in the audience to make a challenging statement or for someone to ask a question. As part of concluding conclusively, return to your chair immediately, radiating confidence and poise all the way. If there is further discussion for you to take part in, it's far better for you to stand up again. Otherwise you are likely to stand there in dead silence waiting for something to happen that doesn't happen, and you then have to sit down on failure all because what you were expecting to happen, didn't.

THE POSITIVE REWARDS

You Can Learn to Think, Speak, and Act Under Pressure

Look at impromptu speaking as another tool to help build additional self-confidence, which carries over to every phase of everyday life. When a man or woman learns to think clearly speaking impromptu, he or she is learning to handle even bigger challenges of life. By using a strong, positive attitude together with the guidelines I have set forth in this chapter, you'll be amazed how you can get your views and ideas across successfully speaking impromptu. Nothing replaces actual experience and practice. Each impromptu speech you give will make the next one a little easier and you'll gradually build your effectiveness. After doing it a few times, when the chairperson or company president says, "Does anyone else have anything to offer pro or con," you'll never sit back and silently say to yourself, "Let Mary or John do it." You'll be the one who stands up and effectively gets your thoughts over. As a result, you'll gain additional recognition, enhance your image, and earn the respect of your listeners. You'll be a leader in demand. These are the positive rewards of effective impromptu speaking.

"GARDLINES"

1. You can think as well on your feet as you can on your seat.
2. The odds are one to a thousand that you will ever be asked to speak impromptu on an unfamiliar subject.

3. The secret to successful impromptu speaking is to speak on specific illustrations, experiences and examples out of your past that you are fully knowledgeable on, either by experience or through past study, and that you have a desire to have other people know about.
4. Here are the guidelines to follow so that you'll sound competent, eloquent and polished.
   a. Quickly define your view-point, or determine the one, definite, purpose of your speech.
   b. Now choose a specific illustration, experience or example.
   c. Start strong.
   d. Don't try to cover too much ground.
   e. Don't apologize anytime.
   f. Conclude conclusively.
5. You can learn to think clearly under pressure.
6. Each impromptu speech will make the next one a little easier.
7. Impromptu speaking is another opportunity to help you gain recognition, enhance your image and earn the respect of your listeners.
8. People who speak well impromptu are usually leaders in demand.

THOUGHT-PROVOKING QUOTES

The measure of the creator
is the amount of life he
puts into his work.
Carl Van Doren

That which does not kill
me makes me stronger.
Friedrich Nietzsche

Our deeds determine us, as
much as we determine our
deeds.
George Eliot

The only thrill worth
while is the one that comes
from making something
out of yourself.
William Feather

Simplicity is making the
journey of this life with
just baggage enough.
Charles Dudley Warner

It is only when
you are pursued
that you become swift.
Kahlil Gibran

Courage is the thing; all
goes if courage goes.
JAMES BARRIE

One of the criteria of
emotional maturity is
having the ability to deal
constructively with reality.
WILLIAM C. MENNINGER

Any man who has a job
has a chance.
ELBERT HUBBARD

I believe that man will
not merely endure; he will
prevail . . . because he has
a soul, a spirit capable
of compassion and sacrifice
and endurance.
WILLIAM FAULKNER

Don't let ambition get so
far ahead that it loses
sight of the job at hand.
WILLIAM FEATHER

Fear nothing, for every
renewed effort raises all
former failures into lessons,
all sins into experience.
KATHERINE TINGLEY

Sometimes a noble failure
serves the world as faithfully
as a distinguished success.
EDWARD DOWDEN

If you want to succeed you
should strike out on new
paths rather than travel the
worn paths of accepted
success.
JOHN D. ROCKEFELLER

13

HOW TO EARN THE EXTRA ADVANTAGE

If you resolutely determined to make a lawyer of yourself, the thing is more than half done already. Always bear in mind that your own resolution to succeed is more important than any other one thing.

ABRAHAM LINCOLN

Victory Over Oneself Is the Greatest Achievement of All

HOW TO GENERATE POSITIVE, POWERFUL INNER MOTIVATION

The Greatest Achievement of All—Victory Over Oneself

Men and women were born to succeed, not to fail. Emerson said, "Success depends on a *plus* condition of mind and body, on power of work, on courage." The man or woman who gains a victory over other people is strong; but the man or woman who gains victory over himself or herself is truly powerful. Mark 9:23, "All things are possible to him that believeth."

It is indeed pitiful seeing and listening to so many people who say they want to become more confident and effective in public speaking, and yet they are not willing to put forth the courage and ambition to make their wishes become reality. So many people start out an undertaking such as this with a half-hearted desire and a weak attitude. After two or three *less than glowingly successful* attempts to speak in public, they give up. They make up some excuse for their short-comings and convince themselves that they weren't cut out for public speaking. We either produce *desired results* or *excuses* in everything we do and there's no in-between. Making up excuses is, of course, the easiest thing to do. Making up excuses is the negative approach, whether it is attempting to become an effective speaker or for anything else worthwhile in life. *In learning to speak confidently and effectively in public, everything you do must be done as if your life depended upon it.* It must be done with a *positive attitude* and a *deep burning desire to succeed.*

Frederick B. Robinson said, "I believe that intense purpose, the moral integrity, the self loyalty that makes a man carry through whatever he undertakes, is the biggest single factor in fitting his mind for great accomplishments" *You can be a confident and effective public speaker.* You must constantly do the very best you can with what you have. Make a firm commitment to yourself and promise yourself you will succeed and don't let anyone or anything stop you.

Have a strong, intense purpose to succeed in public speaking and above all else, by loyal to yourself. There is only one real failure in life and that is not to be true to the best one knows. Harry Emerson Fosdick said, "Rebellion against your handicaps gets you nowhere. Self-pity gets you nowhere. One must have the adventurous daring to accept oneself as a bundle of possibilities and undertake the most interesting game in the world—making the most of one's best." There's only one person you can cheat in the whole world and that is yourself!

Get Excited About Yourself

You've got everything it takes to get what you genuinely and sincerely want. *That's exciting!* Your progress in becoming a confident and effective public speaker is in your hands. No one can do it for you. *Know yourself and believe in yourself.* Become *enthusiastic* about yourself. Work and practice every principle in this book until it becomes habit. Good speaking habits not only train your mind for effective speaking, but for every part of your personal and professional life as well. *That's the extra advantage!*

Form Positive Mind Pictures

You have *inner generating power* to overcome negative, fearful obstacles. *The more urgent your true desire, the faster your progress.* Also, form positive mind pictures in which you see yourself achieving your speaking goals one step at a time. *Keep your mind on the good, positive things that you really want and never on the negative things that you don't want.* This produces positive, powerful inner motivation that will keep you from placing serious, negative limitations on your ability to become an effective speaker. Positive mind pictures and true desire give you an inner strength to shake loose your chains of restraint and help you to break mental barriers. Whatever your mind can conceive and believe it will achieve!

The powerful inner motivating force that comes from true desire and positive mind pictures can make the difference between failing at speaking or succeeding, the difference between being a stock clerk or an executive, or between being a nobody and a professional.

The man or lady who accomplishes anything worthwhile is one who does the *right things right* and who goes after his or her objective like a cat going after a bird in a cage, with intense eagerness and a genuine, determined attitude. The Bible tells us, "If thou faint in the day of adversity, thy strength is small." No rule for success will work if you won't. *Speaking success is achieved by ONLY those who WORK and TRY.*

HOW TO BE PROUD AND STAND OUT OVER THE MASSES

Consider Every Experience a Success

William Whewell's statement about handling hurdles, challenges and failures expresses it so well. He said, "Every failure is a step to success; every detection of what is false directs us toward what is true; every trial exhausts some tempting form of error. Not only so, but scarcely any attempt is entirely a failure; scarcely any theory, the result of steady thought, is altogether false; no attempting form of error is without some latent charm derived from truth."

The most important thing in speaking or in any phase of life is not only to capitalize on your successes, but, equally as important, to be able to profit and to learn from your experiences that are less than successful. Our greatest glories in life do not come from never falling, but in rising every time we fall.

Consider Every Surmounted Problem a Personal Victory

Every profession has problems and challenges. It's good that there are many problems and challenges to overcome in becoming that confident and effective public speaker you really want to become! Why? First, only the courageous and strong hearted will succeed in doing the things necessary to bring about success. Thus they get a super, select reward, *THE EXTRA ADVANTAGE*. Second, every time you surmount a problem, that experience becomes a *personal victory* and you can give yourself a pat on the back and be genuinely and sincerely proud of yourself. You will stand out head and shoulders over the masses!

Every time you have a *personal victory* over a challenge and problem, you take another step up your ladder of success and become that much closer to your total success. The rung of a ladder was never meant to rest upon, but only to hold a person's foot just long enough to enable him or her to put the other foot on a higher rung! With each *personal victory* you become better, wiser, more confident, and more experienced. With every *personal victory* you realize more and more you can control your thoughts, you can choose whether or not your attitude will be positive or negative and that you can accomplish your goals successfully with a strong, burning desire and a positive attitude. This is why I have stressed many times in this book that public speaking is far more than just public speaking. The by-products of successful public speaking are as valuable, and maybe even more so, as the product itself. Successful public speaking requires the development and use of all inner qualities that enable a man or woman to get to the top. These qualities elevate them in their job or profession and also help them to get the most out of life

Public speaking is the fastest and most efficient way that I know of for a person to develop additional courage and self-confidence, a genuine belief in himself or herself. Emerson said, "Self-trust is the first secret of success." Public speaking helps one to develop and to have that self-trust and assists one to become a very self-disciplined person. This in turn helps him or her to form good working and living habits that are beneficial every minute of life. Since habits become power, you'll have just that much more of The Extra Advantage working for you. You'll stand over the masses!

THE PRICE OF SUCCESS IS
PERSEVERENCE . . . FAILURE COMES CHEAPER

Bring Your Do-How Up to Your Know-How

I have attempted to give the beginner or the seasoned Pro a solid track to run on of things to do and things not to do to bring about your speaking success. It will take several readings of this book to grasp all of the material. It will take a great amount of practice and the perseverence making of a good many speeches for you to effectively use, *In your own individual way,* all of the techniques I have shared with you. I promise you there is only one way to achieve your public speaking goal and that is the perseverence of *practice, practice* and more *practice. There is absolutely nothing that is going to take the place of practice and actually giving your speeches to bring your DO-HOW up to your KNOW-HOW.* You must be persistent and learn by doing.

HOW TO KEEP "PUBLIC ENEMY NUMBER 1"
UNDER CONTROL

Don't Run from Stage Fright

I sincerely hope that through this book I can help you turn every speaking experience into a personal victory, and that every personal victory will carry with it the true excitement and enthusiasm that comes from growth and from doing something a little bit better than you did it the last time. Each speaking experience will be easier because you will be learning each time how to better control audience fear, stage fright. Actual experience is the only teacher. You'll be a little more effective each time and you'll lose some excessive self-consciousness with each experience. Don't run from stage fright but have the courage to meet it head-on!

Successful people do things necessary to bring about their success. They don't necessarily like to do some things, but they know they have to if they are going to succeed. Thomas H. Huxley said, "Perhaps the most valuable result of all education is the ability to make yourself do the thing you have to do, when it ought to be done, whether you like it or not. It is the first lesson that ought to be learned." You must do all things that are necessary to bring about your speaking success even if you are afraid to do them!

HOW TO POP UP . . . RIGHT ON TOP

Don't Be Discouraged by Mistakes

By having the right type of attitude and the burning desire to succeed, you have virtually eliminated all big mistakes. You are human and once in a while you may make a small mistake. Don't get discouraged. Mistakes are growing opportunities. You must be willing to accept a mistake now and then.

Risking a mistake is simply the price you pay for speaking success. Look at it this way, each mistake is bringing you a little bit closer to your total goal achievement. There's no doubt that risking a mistake takes courage, but consider the consequences—lack of courage guarantees failure.

T. Ben Allen authored a poem that nicely sums up my attitude, and I hope you will adopt it as yours, about how to handle discouragement and adversities. Mr. Allen is deceased. His daughter, Mrs. E. K. Reed, an outstanding citizen of Omaha, was kind enough to give me permission to include this expressive work.

STAY IN THERE SLUGGING

I'd rather be punched on the end of the nose
Than be kicked in the seat of the pants.
I'd rather walk into a couple of blows
With my head up in fighting advance
Than to hang on the ropes with a sag in my chin
And a hope that I wouldn't get hit,

I prefer to keep going and wading right in;
At least I'd be doing my bit!

I'd rather be known as a man who will plunge
Whatever the odds he is facing
Than be listed as one who will toss in the sponge
When it looks like he's in for a lacing.
I want all my friends to know I am game
And have enough guts to keep SLUGGING
And all that I ask to have after my name
Is "At least the old boy kept plugging."

Life does not always consist in holding a good hand, but in playing a bad hand well. Regardless of how discouraged you might get when speaking problems and mistakes pop up, read that poem and stay in there slugging. You'll pop up, right on top! You are never beaten unless you think you are and you give up. Your attitude determines whether mistakes and defeats are stepping stones or stumbling blocks. You have that decision to make.

DON'T TALK ABOUT IT—DO IT

Never Take Your Mind Off of Your Speaking Goal

If you haven't written out your speaking goal, do it now. Make sure it is realistic and worthy. Put it into action immediately and see yourself enthusiastically achieving your goal successfully. Be sure and put a deadline on your goal, as that blocks out procrastination and gives you a checking point to make sure things are happening on schedule. Never take your mind off of your speaking goal. Keep it before you constantly. Goals are achieved by those who "stay in there slugging."

When you see yourself succeeding in your mind and, you truly feel yourself succeeding in your heart, you will achieve your speaking goal.

You can become a confident and effective public speaker

and when you do, you'll have earned The Extra Advantage and its many rewards.

My conclusive close is the title of my first book: "Don't Talk About it—DO IT!"

"GARDLINES"

Since this is the final summary, I'm listing my final conclusions from over twenty-five years of experience of training men and women to speak in public and from my career as a professional speaker. These points are not listed in any kind of importance.

1. Public speaking is definitely a shortcut to distinction and recognition.
2. The person who has something to say and knows how to say it will stand out and rise way above the common person.
3. The fastest way to overcome fear and to gain additional self-confidence is through mastering public speaking.
4. Any person can develop the ability to be a confident and influential speaker provided he or she properly prepares, practices, has a positive attitude, and a burning desire to succeed.
5. You must know yourself, know your audience, and know your speech.
6. Everything you do must be done as though your life depended on it.
7. Stage fright is nothing to be ashamed of. You can learn to control it. It can be made to work for you instead of against you.
8. You must develop your own speaking style. To try to imitate someone else is nothing short of suicide.
9. Enthusiasm is vital for your success.
10. Most people would rather believe that public speaking is impossible to do rather than pay the price to do it successfully.
11. The only remedy for turning speaking problems into achievements is direct, positive action.
12. If you aren't ready for opportunity, you'll never capitalize on it. It pays to dig the well before you are thirsty.
13. Public speaking is so much more than just public speaking. The

techniques and principles used for developing public speaking skills can be used very successfully in everyone's personal or professional life.

14. No rule for success will work if you won't.

15. Gifted speakers are made, not born.

16. Every person has what it takes to get what he or she wants.

17. You do not need to be a professional speaker or a great orator to make a successful speech . . . but you do have to be properly prepared.

18. Every time you surmount a speaking problem, that experience becomes a personal victory.

19. Effective speaking can be learned only by perseverance and practice.

20. Being a confident and effective public speaker is truly having earned *the extra advantage.*

THOUGHT-PROVOKING QUOTES

The highest reward that God gives us for good work is the ability to do better.
Elbert Hubbard

The greatest test of courage is to beat defeat without losing heart.
ROBERT INGERSOLL

Excellence is everything. Because mediocrity is nothing.
JAMES D. DONOVAN

One cannot be pulled up to a great height. Only a short distance can you be lifted by your arms. But by climbing with your feet and stepping on solid ground below, you can climb mountains.
LOUIS D. BRANDEIS

Don't expect to build up the weak by pulling down the strong.
CALVIN COOLIDGE

The best bet is to bet on yourself.
ARNOLD GLASGOW

I believe that any man's life will be filled with constant and unexpected encouragement, if he makes up his mind to do his level best each day, and as nearly as possible reach the high-water mark of pure and useful living.
BOOKER T. WASHINGTON

Most of us expect too
much from others and
not enough from ourselves.
WILLIAM FEATHER

God intends no man to live
in this world without working;
but it seems to me no less'
evident that HE intends every
man to be happy in his work.
JOHN RUSKIN

There is, in addition to a
courage with which men die,
a courage by which men must
live.
JOHN F. KENNEDY

He who stops being better,
stops being good.
OLIVER CROMWELL

Let no man delude himself
by the belief that the good
things of life will endure
through the sheer quality
of their goodness.
RALPH BARTON PERRY

My father taught me to work,
but not to love it. I never
did like to work, and I don't
deny it. I'd rather read, tell
stories, crack jokes, talk
laugh—anything but work.
ABRAHAM LINCOLN

Be satisfied with your
business, and learn to love
what you were bred to do.
MARCUS AURELIUS